Canada

Alan Seale has an amazing talent to explain the transformation journey in a way that is accessible to all. Reading his words gives us hope that together we can indeed create a world that works.

—Stephane Leblanc, CEO
International Centre for Conscious Leadership

I have been an avid follower of thought leader Alan Seale for the past number of years and have been eagerly anticipating this latest book. Alan's current messages resonate with me and with those readers who also want to make a difference in the world—a world that is indeed, as Alan says, "breaking open." Alan provides a space for people to thrive as we become more skilled in TransformActional work.

—Laurie Hillis
MA in Leadership, PCC, Coach Supervisor
Master Facilitator, Brave Leaders Inc.

Costa Rica

For all those who are committed to making a change in their world—our world—this book could not be more timely. Not only does Alan Seale have an amazing capacity for deeply understanding life as energy in motion and making sense of our complex world, he also has a unique ability to communicate this to others in a simple, clear, and concise way that can be understood and integrated into our daily lives.

—Karen Montealegre
Founder and Director of Alter Equus

Denmark

The body of Alan Seale's work continues to come together as THE platform for a sustainable future and a way of living, leading, and serving. His latest book, Transformational Presence, is a great invitation not to wait for something to happen—it is up to you and me more than ever to act and do something now. This book is full of hope, positive impact, and great inspiration—a must read for anyone looking for new perspectives about how to lead in a VUCA world.

—Michael Skjoet
Founder and Director Skjoet-Consulting and
Executive Coaching

Germany

As a committed change-maker who is both distracted and disconcerted by current events, I found Transformational Presence: How To Make a Difference In a Rapidly Changing World, well, utterly transformational. This book literally reintroduced me to myself on a deep soul level. Alan Seale illuminates a new way of living and leading which combines both the knowledge of the head and the intuition of the heart to build a strong foundation for a powerful new way to "show up" in the world. For anyone who wants to engage in the world but may feel paralyzed or stuck, this book couldn't be more timely and important.

—Daniel Karslake
Director/Producer/Filmmaker

Alan Seale is the ultimate mastermind, philosopher, and coach for everything connected to the creation and protection of an effective future in business and life. His out-of-the-box thinking and even his easily understandable quantum physics perspectives focus the reader's thinking on the most fundamental essence: energy. Alan Seale offers us true next-level thinking and outstanding leadership and life technology.

—Hans Neff
Executive Coach and Mentor

The Netherlands

In eloquent, simple, yet powerful language, Alan Seale opens a challenging and inspiring door to the essence of leadership that's needed in our complex and uncertain world. For anyone who wants to make a difference in the world, this book will be a powerful beacon of light to show you step by step the way to navigate through the deep complexities of the society we are living in at the moment. For Transformational Presence alumni, you will have the privilege to be engrossed again in the main concepts of this work and will discover how—with intent— you can transform into a TransformActional leader. Deep respect!

—Sascha Krijger
Organizational Coach and
Consultant in the Not-for-Profit Sector

This book is cutting-edge. It points the way towards the Next Level in Leadership. It's insightful and practical for living and managing in our VUCA world. If you're looking for a way to handle the complexity in your life and business, turn to Transformational Presence. It will give you all you need and much more.

—Sander van Eekelen
Leadership Coach
Founder of the Academy of Life

Transformational Presence represents a new way of working, living, and connecting, offering new language and structures to help us step into the energy of this time. Alan Seale is the living example of a TransformActional Leader in the ways he brings together theory and practice.

—Carina Benninga
Executive Coach and Leader of Bureau Benninga

I love this book! It powerfully brings the concepts of Transformational Presence into the here and now. It addresses exactly what is currently happening in the world and the invitation for leaders globally at this moment. Through Alan's Three Fundamental Questions and many other tools and concepts, together we can co-create new structures to bring alive the emerging potential in the world. This book shows us how to co-create with the potential—not just bring brilliant new ideas, but also create new systems and structures that will serve that emerging potential and embed these structures into business, organizations, and society.

—Maarten van Neerven
Chief Financial Officer, Bugaboo

Poland

In an era where it's clear that the old, power-based leadership models either fail or make people unhappy, Alan's concepts provide comprehensive, proven alternative models based on seeing the world around us through the perspective of energy and in balance between our intellect and intuition. A must-read for all transformational leaders, strategists and innovators!

—Maciej Szturmowicz, MBA
Change Integrator and Entrepreneur
Advisor to the Management Board of mBank S.A.

Alan Seale takes us on a deep dive into the concept of life and leadership as energy in motion. He invites us to live at the crossroads of Presence and Action. This book offers simple and approachable yet powerful and transformative support for New Generation Leaders. It calls us to make some effort; to take in what Alan offers, we need new eyes. We must look beyond the obvious and step beyond the comfort of our "known" world. This is not just a book to read; it's a message to become. It's a living and breathing invitation to choose the path least followed in order to prepare a gateway for many more who are waiting at the horizon.

—Joanna Zawada - Kubik
Executive and Organizational Coach

Romania

When I first met Alan Seale in 2009, his work was difficult for me to accept because of my years of education and conditioning to make things happen and to control outcomes. Through working with Alan, I was in time able to let go of attachment to outcomes and focus on intention. Things started changing in my work. As time went on, I was able to start practicing a more transformational framework. And this is the approach I use in coaching managers now. In reading Alan's latest book, many remaining parts of what he teaches are starting to make sense to me. What I understand now is that the brain knows, the heart understands. Through using Alan's simple yet profoundly deep approach in letting the potential lead the way, you will finally understand yourself.

—Serban Chinole
Executive Coach for Senior Managers in Transition
Founder of Coaching Attic

Sweden

Read this book now and then give it to the first fellow human you can think of. Be a Voyager when you read it and embrace its message for you. Use your heart in cooperation with your brain. We can make a world that works possible together.

—Britt Weide, MCC
Coach Supervisor, and Certified Transformational Presence Coach
Director of Training at CoachWalk Academy

Switzerland

Transformational Presence is an inspirational read for those in the world that work at the edges. It connects the dots from what Alan calls the "Great Breaking Open" towards a holistic concept of "Transform-Actional leadership"—a new kind of leadership that many of us are striving for. I can't wait to read the companion book with specific tools, skills and frameworks for next-level "TransformAction."

—Jan Maisenbacher
Founder WICKEDPROJECTS

United Kingdom

A book that makes my heart sing: full of practical wisdom for all those who want to express their soul purpose and make a difference in the world. Highly recommended.

—Richard Barrett
Chairman of the Barrett Values Centre
Founder of the Academy for the Advancement of Human Values

Written with clarity and compassion, Transformational Presence will challenge and expand the way you think about life, and about the potential that lies within the great challenges – personal, organisational, and political – that beset us today. And it will support you with the tools, approaches, and new perspectives that will allow you first to become a leader in your own life and, in so doing, start making your own contribution to creating a world that works.

For everyone who wants to make a positive contribution, and to thrive and help others thrive in these turbulent times, this book will not only lead you to new insights about where you might start; it will also give you the tools you need to transform those insights into action. Profound and practical.

—James Clark
Clear Coaching & Consulting Ltd

We live in uncertain and unpredictable times. That's not a comfortable place to be if you are a leader. Yet there has never been a greater need for top leaders to step forward and help fashion this world for future generations. It requires a new type of leadership of organisations, of communities, of countries. It requires Transformational Presence. Alan Seale's new book is a gift to our troubled and confused world. If any part of you tells you that you can make a difference, you can. Read this book and make a start.

—Lloyd Wigglesworth
Founder of CEO Coaching

USA

Alan's latest book provides hope and a big vision for a world that feels overwhelmingly divided and unjust. Drawing on ancient wisdom traditions, quantum physics, and complexity theory, Alan disrupts traditional leadership paradigms with a set of new and powerful tools that have the potential to bring us all closer together and give us the results we need in times of uncertainty and complexity.

—Kathrin O'Sullivan
Executive Coach & Consultant
Former Head of Executive Development at Google

For those ready to step up and into heightened awareness, this book will guide you to a deeper understanding of who you are and how you show up, and give you a means to express your inner gifts through your leadership and service. If this book has crossed your path, the invitation has been extended. It is your choice to be open and curious. By opening your mind and inviting your heart, I have no doubt the messages conveyed through Alan Seale will touch you deeply and offer tools and techniques to ignite a new way of being.

—Jayne L. Garrett, PCC
Author, Coach, Facilitator Leadership Development

TRANSFORMATIONAL PRESENCE

How To Make a Difference
In a Rapidly Changing World

TRANSFORMATIONAL PRESENCE

How To Make a Difference
In a Rapidly Changing World

ALAN SEALE

Center for
Transformational Presence

First published in 2017 by
The Center for Transformational Presence
P.O. Box 61
Topsfield, MA 01983
www.transformationalpresence.org

Library of Congress Control Number 2017956363

Cover design by Kandy Tobias
Book design by Kandy Tobias

ISBN: 978-0-9825330-2-4

*To the Transformational Presence community
with deep love, gratitude, admiration, and respect
for the many ways you are helping to
create a world that works.*

CONTENTS

Making a Difference In a Rapidly Changing World

There is a vitality, a life force, a quickening,
that is translated through you into action,
and because there is only one of you in all of time,
this expression is unique.
And if you block it,
it will never exist through any other medium
and it will be lost.
The world will not have it.
It is not your business to determine how good it is
nor how valuable
nor how it compares with other expressions.
It is your business to keep it yours
clearly and directly, to keep the channel open.
You do not even have to believe in yourself or your work.
You have to keep yourself open and aware to the urges that motivate you.
Keep the channel open.
No artist is pleased.
There is no satisfaction at any time.
There is only a queer divine dissatisfaction,
a blessed unrest that keeps us marching
and makes us more alive than the others.

—Martha Graham,
choreographer and pioneer of modern dance

WE LIVE IN A RAPIDLY changing world. In fact, change is happening at a pace never before seen in human history, and that pace is likely to keep getting faster. Because there are more and more moving pieces and things are less and less clearly defined, uncertainty has become the new normal.

Some might say that everything is breaking down and falling apart. Yet what if things are actually breaking *open* so that everything that has been hidden or does not serve a greater good for all can be revealed? What if things are breaking open so that we can make a fresh start—so that something new can be created? What if big things are waiting to happen? What if we are at a tipping point for creating a world that works?

Chances are that you, like me, feel called to make a difference in this rapidly changing world, or you wouldn't have been drawn to this book. Years ago, modern dance pioneer and choreographer Martha Graham spoke the words that begin this Introduction to choreographer Agnes de Mille (Agnes de Mille, p. 264). Today, more people than ever are feeling their own "divine dissatisfaction" or "blessed unrest" and want to make a difference. Yet also, unfortunately, it's easy to get bogged down in not knowing how or where to begin.

It's OK that you don't know. Just start. Start where you are, and start now. It doesn't matter as much *where* you begin as it does that you just begin. As you do, things will start to happen, and a path will begin to reveal itself. This is the new world. We discover and create as we go, working with what we have and manifesting what we don't have. Step by step, things unfold and, through the process, we learn how to do what we need to do. This book will help you get started.

I wrote this book for people who are committed to making a difference—people who have not just a desire, but a drive or passion within them for being of service towards a greater good. This book is for visionaries who want to get beyond their vision into action. It's for leaders who seek support in navigating the unknown and pioneering new territory. It's for coaches who support people in living into their greatest potential and bringing their gifts to the world. It's for teachers who are looking for simple yet powerful language and structure to make big concepts accessible and applicable for all. It's for people who have dedicated significant portions of their lives to serving others. And it's for anyone who wants to help create a world that works.

The Transformational Presence approach might not be what you would expect to find in a "how-to" book. You will not find a ten-step plan or process. You will not find a magic formula that makes all things happen. That's because linear, detailed, step-by-step plans and formulas often don't work very well anymore. However, what you *will* find are simple, practical, and powerful approaches that can serve you no matter what your project or challenge may be.

This book is actually the first of a two-part *Transformational Presence* set. It begins by offering a fundamental understanding of what Transformational Presence is and the role it can play in today's world. From there, we explore how life works as energy in motion and how that can help us in these times of rapid change and deep uncertainty. Through this exploration, you will learn more about how to navigate this unpredictable, complex, and often confusing world. Finally, we prototype a new kind of leadership—a leadership that serves us going forward in the most powerful, productive, effective, and impactful ways—a leadership that can support us in navigating new territories and learning to thrive in new creative spaces and new ways of being.

In the second book, *Transformational Presence: The Tools, Skills, and Frameworks,* we continue to prototype this new leadership through more than forty simple, powerful, and practical tools, frameworks, skills, models, and approaches that are designed specifically for our rapidly changing times. You can begin applying them immediately in your life, leadership, and service. They are effective in all kinds of settings—with individuals, families, classrooms, teams, organizations, and companies.

This first book will expand your thinking, perception, awareness, and understanding. Then the *Frameworks* book will help you discover "how" to do whatever needs to be done *as you do it.* These two books together are also the primary resource books for our newest Leadership Development programs (TransformationalPresence.org).

While there is an intentional linear flow throughout this book, I have also written each chapter so that it can stand alone. Therefore, as you look at the Table of Contents, if you are drawn to a particular chapter topic right away, it's OK to start there. Then keep reading the chapters in the order that they call out to you.

To get the most out of this book, I also encourage you to share it with your friends and colleagues. You might want to organize a discussion group to explore the book chapter by chapter and share insights and discoveries. You will also find video and audio resources and other supports at TransformationalPresenceBook.com.

Before we dive into the first chapter, perhaps it is helpful to clarify what I mean by "a world that works." Within the context of all that is happening today, it can be difficult to imagine that such a world could be possible. If we think of a world that works as a specific result or outcome, then to create that world is a daunting task indeed. However, if we remember that transformation happens through process, and that it happens from the inside out, then creating a world that works becomes about process and ways of living, being, and doing, not about outcomes. These are concepts that we will explore in the coming chapters.

Large-scale societal transformation happens as a result of transformational shifts over time at the grassroots level. It's an ongoing and ever-evolving process that happens one person, one family, one organization, one company, and one country at a time. It unfolds through conversations with the people around us, especially when we create spaces where it is safe to be open and honest, to be curious and to explore, and to listen without judgment.

Societal transformation comes alive in those moments when we recognize ourselves in other people who we always thought were different from us. It's awakened when we spend time in the beauty and wonder of nature, turning off devices and conversation and just being present with the natural world. It unfolds through shared experience, both joyful and tragic, and through exchanging ideas with colleagues and friends. It expands through discussion groups in houses of worship, social clubs, and the corner café or bar. Over time, we reach a tipping point and recognize that a shift in consciousness has occurred. Again, it's a process.

In the end, the only way we will find out whether or not our visions can become reality is to commit to them and start taking steps towards manifesting them. For me, what I describe in these next few paragraphs gives a sense of direction and fundamental purpose for my work in the world.

When I speak of a world that works, I don't mean a perfect world. Actually, I don't believe that there is supposed to be such a thing. I believe that our most fundamental reason for living is to learn. If everything was perfect, what would be the need for learning? On both individual and societal levels, we are all on different learning curves. Some are steep—at times they may even feel insurmountable. Other learning curves feel gentler and easier to climb. None of us can truly know what others are experiencing on the inside—their struggles, fears, challenges, and opportunities. However, though our outer circumstances may be very different, what we experience on the inside is more similar than we might imagine.

Years ago, one of my first life teachers often said, "We all have the same hundred lessons to learn. It's just that we learn them in different sequences." So while I'm working on lesson number 23, you might be on lesson 58. While one family is working through challenges of survival because of lack of educational opportunities and financial resources, another family is faced with learning how to be good stewards of their wealth. While one country is struggling with the most basic human rights issues, another country has established those basic freedoms, yet is working through less obvious, yet very real, racial, gender, and class issues.

Regardless of who we are and where we live, we are all in a process of learning. In areas of life where some of us are doing quite well, others may be struggling. And what others have mastered, we may find challenging. In a world that works, we acknowledge the challenges that come with learning, growth, and development, and stand committed to working *with* one another instead of against one another.

When I imagine a world that works, I imagine a world

where we talk with one another. Perhaps even more importantly, we *listen* to one another. We communicate openly between cultures, governments, and businesses. We are willing to hear and consider different ideas, approaches, value systems, and ways of thinking, and we all understand that no one has the whole truth. It takes the perspectives of everyone involved to be able to see the entire picture.

In those dialogues, we accept that sometimes it will be easy to find the common goal and a path that everyone can agree on. At other times, there will be disagreement and conflict. After all, the many people and cultures of the world hold vastly different value structures and are in different places in their own evolutionary process. Therefore, each individual and each culture is learning different lessons and working through different issues at different times. I learned a long time ago that peace is not the absence of conflict, yet it can be how we choose to *respond* to the conflict.

In a world that works, there is an understanding that everything is interconnected and therefore, everything impacts everything else. There is a common understanding that the wellbeing of one is ultimately dependent on the wellbeing of all. Because of that understanding, we have a shared commitment to finding a way of living and working together where everyone gets at least some of the help, support, information, knowledge, and understanding they need, and where no choices or decisions are made at the expense of others.

In a world that works, we are willing to be present with both joy and pain as a natural part of life, within ourselves and in others. We take personal, business, and government integrity seriously and accept responsibility for our choices and actions, both those that turned out well and those that we regret. We acknowledge which choices and actions served a greater good and which ones served only a select few. And from that awareness, we seek to make choices that serve something bigger than ourselves—to serve more than only our own interests.

In a world that works, we create societal and organizational cultures where exploration, discovery, creativity, and innovation are encouraged and supported. At the same time, there is a general understanding and acceptance that when we are trying something new, it will not always turn out as we had hoped. We create a space where it is safe to learn.

In a world that works, there is also a common understanding that everything will not change overnight. In fact, some things may take many years—even many generations—to be accomplished. Consider the beautiful cathedrals of Europe or many of the ancient sacred temples and sanctuaries of the world. Many of them took more than a hundred years to build. Those who were a part of a project's beginning had no expectation of seeing it finished in their lifetimes. The artisans and craftsmen just focused on doing their part in the creation of something that they hoped would be beautiful, inspiring, and uplifting to those who would visit in the future. They took great pride in their work and in their contribution to the realization of a bigger vision.

Futurist Ari Wallach calls this "Longpath" (longpath. org)—a practice made up of three transformative ways of thinking.

The first is "transgenerational thinking"—thinking beyond our lifetime and considering the impacts on generations to come. This idea is not new. Native American traditions have taught us to consider the impact of our actions and decisions on seven generations into the future. However, because of our current obsession with what Wallach calls "short-termism," transgenerational thinking feels like a new idea.

The second of his three transformative ways of thinking is "futures thinking." Ari Wallach points out that, as a culture, when we think about the future, our first thoughts often go to the evolution of technology and what might become possible in that future world. While technology is certainly important, Wallach reminds us that there are also other "futures" to consider. For example, how might our sense of ethics and morality evolve? What is the future of families and social systems? What is the future of compassion and human relations? What about the futures of faith and art? Wallach reminds us that we have many futures to imagine, not just a future based on technology.

Finally, there is "*telos* thinking." The Greek word *telos* means "ultimate aim" or "ultimate purpose." With whatever endeavor we are engaged, *telos* thinking invites us to consider one simple yet powerful question: To what end are we doing this? In other words, what will be different by taking this step, changing this policy, or shifting this approach? What will come after? And not just a year from now or even five years from now. What will have happened 20, 50, or 100 years from now because we made this choice today?

In a world that works, the concept of Longpath is part of the mainstream conversation. It is accepted that some projects will be completed within months or a few years, while others will take much longer. Leaders, organizations, corporations, and governments are expected to have a Longpath vision. In planning and policy discussions, "To what end?" is a standard question. In a world that works, society as a whole expects choices to be made and actions to be taken in service of the Longpath view for the greater good of all.

Making a difference in the world begins with being willing to be fully present with the invitations, opportunities, challenges, and complexities that are in front of us. Then, as best we can, we get to the core or essence of what is happening and begin working from the inside out. From there, we move forward in powerful, effective, and sustainable action. These two books show you how.

I believe that life is driven by an evolutionary force and intelligence—first, a force for survival, and then an intelligence that can support us to thrive. Look at the resilience of nature. New growth comes within weeks after a forest fire. Wildflowers, grasses, shrubs, and even trees grow out of rocky cliffs. Left to its own process, life *will* find a path forward. Life will carry us. In the evolutionary process, there is always the next potential waiting to unfold. However, it's up to us to learn how to *work with* that evolutionary intelligence and its powerful flow rather than try to manipulate outcomes by *pushing against* the natural and evolutionary process.

This is not a new message. However, it's a truth that we easily forget when faced with challenges and uncertainty. We are conditioned to push against what is "not working" instead of looking for the "intelligence" or "message" that is trying to get our attention through our circumstance. There is always a wave to ride, a potential to follow, something wanting to happen next. It's the natural flow—the instinct of life for survival, and, ultimately, for thriving.

There is something that "wants to happen" in the world through you. Whatever your vision or calling—whatever the contribution you are here to make—let this book and its companion help you do it. We are at a tipping point. The world can't afford for you to wait any longer. The time to put our focus on creating a world that works is now.

CHAPTER 1

Why Transformational Presence? Why Now?

One of the most calming and powerful actions
you can do to intervene in a stormy world
is to stand up and show your soul.
Soul on deck shines like gold in dark times.
The light of the soul throws sparks, can send up flares, builds signal fires…
causes proper matters to catch fire.
To display the lantern of soul in shadowy times like these—
to be fierce and to show mercy toward others, both—
are acts of immense bravery and greatest necessity.
Struggling souls catch light from other souls
who are fully lit and willing to show it.
If you would help to calm the tumult,
this is one of the strongest things you can do.

—Clarissa Pinkola Estés
("Letter To a Young Activist During Troubled Times")

WE BEGIN WITH A STORY of Transformational Presence that captures what this work is all about.

A man came to see me for a coaching session. We were meeting for the first time. Although he was a man of great accomplishment and the president and CEO of a highly respected company, right now he was clearly feeling shaken. Within the first few minutes, he said, "I feel like the ground underneath my feet is shifting. There is no firm place to stand; nothing feels secure; nothing feels predictable and safe." He looked down in silence. For a first conversation, we were already in deep.

After a moment, I asked, "So what's going on inside of you?"

"It's not exactly scary," he responded hesitantly. "And 'afraid' is not the right word. It feels uncertain, uneasy." He paused for a moment, and then added, "And somehow it's also OK. It surprises me to say that, but right now as I sit here, somehow it feels OK."

"What makes it OK?" I asked.

Again, silence. Then, after a deep and long breath, he said, "I think it's OK because, in the last few days, I'm starting to realize that, deep inside, I'm still who I am—I'm still me—no matter what's happening around me."

There was a palpable shift in the energy in the room. The air was charged with the kind of powerful tension that comes when something big is happening—something is breaking open. We both could feel it, yet there was also an incredible stillness. We were hardly breathing. I recognized that my role in this session was to hold the space for his unfolding discovery. He was already in his own transformation process—I was here to be his witness.

After allowing us both a moment to be with what was happening, I asked, "So who are you, deep inside, no matter what is happening around you?"

There was another long silence, yet I realized that it wasn't because he was searching for an answer. Instead, he seemed to be gathering the courage to actually say out loud what he knew. The air in the room became even more charged as his vulnerability gave way to power and strength—the kind of authentic power and strength that can only come when we are willing to be open and real.

He stood and crossed the room to look out the window. "I know that I have a purpose and that I'm in this situation for a reason. I have an ability to meet groups of people where they are. I'm able to find the best in them, even when they can't. Somehow, I can see them in their greatest strength and can even help them to see that strength in themselves."

He continued gazing out the window. "I don't know how to explain it, but it's as if something happens in the space in between us. Safety. Confidence. Assurance. It's like something bigger than we are is holding us. And in that moment we touch something deep inside of ourselves. It's like, just for a moment, we meet on the soul level." He paused, and then added cautiously, almost under his breath, "Maybe that's what it's all about."

It felt as if time had stopped. All the tension and electricity in the room had suddenly been transformed. There was an unspoken acknowledgement between us that we were touching the power and resilience of the human spirit—the force inside of us that gives us life and breath— the source of being.

He crossed back to the center of the room, letting his own words sink in. "I can't believe that I'm saying all of this. I never knew that saying those words out loud to someone else could be so powerful *and* such a relief. I was taught that leaders didn't say things like that—that it made you look soft and sentimental—and that's not who I was supposed to be if I wanted to be a respected and effective leader.

"But you know what, that kind of leader that I was taught to be—it never felt like who I was. Yes, I can be strong and decisive and create strategies and get people to do big things and accomplish big stuff—I can do all of that. Yet right now I'm feeling more powerful than I've ever felt in my life. And I'm realizing that my real power doesn't come from all those things I can do. My real power comes from the space I create for people to thrive."

He came back to his chair. "Nothing has changed on the outside, but everything has changed on the inside. And I've touched a power and a force within me that I can never not know again."

After another long silence, he continued quietly, "The ground is still shifting. And it's going to keep shifting. Nothing in my life and work is stable right now, nor is it going to be any time soon. And that's just how it is. Somehow I'm OK with that. I know now that nothing can harm me at my center. I know that I am safe inside of me, no matter what happens on the outside. I've never claimed this for myself before. And when I create that space for others, they can find their safety inside, too.

"Who I am at my center is bigger than my circumstance—bigger than anything that can happen to me. And that's true for all of the people around me, too. And that's the most important thing that I have to offer as a leader. I can create a space that encourages all of us to be our best and to recognize that, together, from the essence of who we are, we are bigger than what is happening around us. I can create a space that opens up possibilities. I can create a space that helps people feel and sense that we're all in this together. That's my job."

He stood, picked up his jacket, and crossed back to gaze out the window once more. After a few moments, he looked at me and said, "We're all in this together. The ground is shifting underneath all of us. And if we take care of each other, we're all going to be OK. Thanks."

≈

A powerful conscious living and leadership movement is now emerging in many parts of the world. It's a movement built on greater conscious awareness, understanding, perception, and transformative action. It's built on the conviction that, in any initiative, all stakeholders can be served, all people *and* the environment can be honored and respected, and economic models can serve something more than just our individual or organizational interests.

Within this movement, there is also widespread agreement that leading the world forward in the most effective, impactful, and transformative ways will require new skills and tools, as well as broader capacities for awareness and perception. These new skills and capacities require us to stretch far beyond the familiar, analytical, knowledge-based, figure-it-out approaches taught in traditional learning environments into more creative, discovery-based, transformational approaches. And this is what Transformational Presence is all about.

Going forward, we need leaders who know how to be fully present with the reality of whatever is happening in the moment—leaders who can feel, sense, and listen to the energy within situations and circumstances and discover what is needed next. We need leaders who can be comfortable in not knowing the answers—and maybe not even knowing the questions. We need curious and imaginative leaders who are willing to explore without knowing what they will find, yet trust that clues for next steps will appear. And we need leaders who, when they sense these next steps, are not afraid to take action.

We need leaders who are "at home in their own skin"— who are comfortable with who they are, and who fully embrace their own talents, skills, and gifts. At the same time, these leaders thrive on continued learning through their leadership experience. They constantly seek to broaden their horizons of understanding and awareness. As they continue to learn and grow, they also create the best possible culture and environment for others to thrive and develop to their greatest potential—to experience their own breakthroughs in understanding, awareness, perception, and action. They create environments where people feel safe to try new things and to learn from their experience, safe to admit that they don't know where to go or what next step to take when everything is changing, and safe to bring their full, authentic selves to the table.

We need leaders who recognize that everything is connected to everything else—who embody the understanding that the world is built on a matrix of relationships, and that everything that happens is a part of a larger flow. Nothing exists in isolation. Everything exists within a larger context.

This is the leadership that will transform our world. It's leadership built not only on a philosophy or a set of ideas or beliefs; it's also built on a particular set of skills, tools, and approaches. It's leadership built on open and expansive worldviews; knowledge of how to navigate unknown territory; and the wisdom to know when to move forward and when to step back, when to take action and when to pause and let things settle. This is Transformational Presence.

Transformational Presence is not a model or a formula. It's a way of living, leading, and serving—an approach that provides a strong foundation for conscious living and conscious leadership. Transformational Presence is also a practical set of skills that, when developed together, build and expand our capacities for awareness, understanding, perception, and effective action—capacities that are essential for navigating today's rapidly changing world.

In the Japanese culture, there is a concept they call *kokoro*, which literally translates to mean "mind, heart, spirit." It's about alignment of energy in your "being." If you want to accomplish something or to have something, the concept of *kokoro* asks, "What are the qualities of the person who would have that or do that?" In other words, if that is what you want to do or have, then who must you be? How you live is how you will lead, coach, serve, teach, and parent. Your worldview colors everything.

In the spirit of *kokoro*, two sets of questions arise as we consider how to carry this conscious living and leadership movement forward:

1. Who do we need to be in order to put these powerful new ideas into place? What qualities do we need to develop within ourselves? How do we need to "show up" to life and leadership?

2. What skills, tools, frameworks, approaches, awareness, and capacities do we need within us as the people who will facilitate transformation going forward, whether in our families and communities, or in business, healthcare, education, politics and government, or social support services?

These questions are at the heart of what Transformational Presence and these two books are all about. The Center for Transformational Presence is a discovery, learning, and transformation environment supporting leaders, coaches, teachers, visionaries, managers, parents, healthcare professionals, public servants, and anyone who wants to make a difference in navigating today's rapidly changing world. We provide virtual learning and in-person workshops, professional and personal development programs, as well as both individual and organizational coaching on a global level.

Our work begins with helping individuals and organizations develop a skill set for *being* a Transformational Presence, for shaping a transformational culture, and for leading transformational initiatives. We begin with a set of tools, models, and structures that together form the Transformational Presence approach. As our participants put those skills and models into practice, they begin to build and expand their inner capacities for awareness, perception, compassion, understanding, and effective action. Their worldviews expand and they begin engaging with the people and situations around them in more dynamic, effective, and impactful ways.

Martin specializes in supporting entrepreneurs. Several years after participating in Transformational Presence programs, he wrote, "Working in the space between 'what is' and 'what could be' comes with many creative tensions for which traditional problem-solving skills no longer work. Transformational Presence has helped me tap into the 'energy of potential' that is contained in these tensions and become a steward for the new opportunities to break through. What started out as a mechanism to change my work has now become a natural and very fulfilling way of life."

Jillian, an executive coach and trainer, says, "Transformational Presence has taught me a way of being and doing that enables me to cut straight to the core of an issue with those I serve, work with whatever appears, and move forward with speed and ease. What once took an hour of coaching now unfolds in twenty minutes. The tools, frameworks, and approaches are hugely powerful in their simplicity, inviting deep insights, new opportunities, and answers to quickly arise, regardless of how complex or emotionally charged the issue is."

Several months after his first Transformational Presence workshop, Ian, a creative arts professional, shared, "This work has allowed me to relax into and find security in the unknown. It's helped turn my fear and frustration into excitement and possibility."

Ingela, a leadership coach, says, "Transformational Presence taught me how to listen and to speak with my 'heart language,' which takes my doing, being, feeling, and thinking to a greater synergetic level."

Sharon, the executive director of a non-profit service organization, says, "Transformational Presence has taught me to operate from a deeper place of listening and connection than ever before. The power of that—the true power of Transformational Presence—has rippled through every element of my agency. In turn, it has deepened our agency's connection to our mission. This depth and drawing out has allowed me to embrace a greater understanding of my presence and my work in the world. I can feel the power of that gift and have been able to extend and embody that in my leadership approach."

Sharon goes on to say, "Finding Transformational Presence has brought new ways of thinking and a new vocabulary to match what I so deeply value. Not a day goes by where the 'centering' and 'practice' of Transformational Presence has not helped ground and lead me back to the truths that inspire and empower me to do my work in the world."

When I first coined the term "Transformational Presence" in the mid-2000s, neither "transformation" nor "presence" was commonly used within everyday conversation. Now, however, both of these words have become a part of mainstream vocabulary, even to the point of overuse in some contexts. When this happens, we risk losing touch with the power that lies in the root meaning of those words. So let's go back to the root meanings.

"Transformation" comes out of the Latin root *transforma*, meaning "change across form." It is a shift at the most fundamental levels of being, thinking, perception, character, and worldview. In quantum physics terms, you could say that transformation is the result of a fundamental shift in vibrational frequency and pattern at the core or essence level. When shifts occur at the core of our being and understanding, then our thoughts and/or beliefs, and often even our circumstances and how we approach them, change to the degree that they can never go back to how they were before. This is because *we* have transformed in some fundamental way.

You have probably experienced this at least once in your life—a moment when something happens and suddenly you understand what is happening in a new or different way. And you realize deep in the heart of your being that you can never go back to where you were before. Some people would call this a paradigm shift. Others might call it a personal transformation. Whatever you may call it, the bottom

line is that once you know something, you can never "not
know" it again. Once you have had a profound experience,
you can never again *not* have had that experience. Something has changed deep within you.

Form follows energy. The form that something takes,
whether that form is a physical object or a circumstance
or situation, is a result of energy organizing itself in a particular way. You could also say that form follows awareness.
Our level of awareness, perception, understanding, and ultimately, our worldview, shapes the forms that we create. We
can easily create outer change by making different decisions
or moving things around. Yet in order for outer change to
be effective and lasting, whether in individuals, families,
organizations, or societies, some inner transformation must
have occurred. If this doesn't make complete sense to you
right now, don't worry. We'll be exploring these ideas more
fully in the pages to come.

"Presence" comes out of the Latin word *praesentia*.
Before the 16th century, *praesentia* meant simply "being
present." However, in the 1500s, the meaning of the word
evolved to "carriage, demeanor, aspect." While many people
think of the word "presence" simply as the act of being present, there is a far greater meaning when it comes to making
a difference in the world. Not only must we be fully present
in the moment; we also need to be aware of the "presence"
that we bring to the "present" moment. How do we "show
up" in our personal relationships, in our families, and with
our friends? How do we "show up" with our colleagues,
with our collaborators, or with those that we lead and serve?
How do we "show up" in daily life out in the world? What
do people feel or sense when they are with us? What does
our presence evoke or call forth in others?

Bringing those two words together, **"Transformational Presence"** means showing up to life and leadership in a way that creates the best possible conditions for transformation to occur. We cannot make transformation happen—that's called "manipulation!" Yet we *can* create environments and cultures that encourage transformation to unfold.

Creating transformational environments and cultures is a bit like tending a garden. When you plant a seed, there is nothing you can do to make that seed grow. However, there are many things you can do to create the best possible *conditions or environment* for that seed to grow. You can plant the seed in rich soil and in a spot where it will get just the right amount of sunlight. You can make sure that the seed gets the right amount of water and nutrients. You can pull the weeds around it so that, as the seed sprouts and begins to grow, the plant has room to breathe and fill out.

Transformational Presence nurtures seeds of potential. This can mean many things, depending on the setting and circumstance. Yet it begins with embodying the principles, concepts, and understanding that you gain through this book. From there, you create an intentional culture and environment where exploration and discovery are encouraged—where it's safe to experiment, even if you don't get the results you had hoped for. You create a space where it's safe to be open and honest, and where there is respect for the human spirit. And then you inspire and empower the people around you to live into their greatest potential.

Transformational Presence approaches open and expand the fundamental ways in which people think, perceive, and understand. When you help those around you develop *new ways* of thinking, then *what* they think will, in turn, expand and evolve. Those new ways of thinking include engaging the intuitive mind and our powerful, built-in heart intelligence. In Transformational Presence, we call it Whole-Mind Thinking and Whole-Being Awareness. Whole-Mind Thinking brings intellect and intuition together into a dynamic and productive partnership. Whole-Body Awareness then expands that partnership even further to include the extraordinary human energy technology available to us through our bodies. We'll be exploring these concepts much more throughout the book, particularly in Chapters 2 and 6.

The tools and approaches you will learn through these two books will help you develop and refine your Whole-Mind Thinking and Whole-Being Awareness skills and capacities. You will learn how to cut through complexity to get to the essence of what is happening and work from the inside out. You will learn how to recognize the potential that is ready and waiting to emerge, how to sense and follow the signals that will show you the way forward, and then how to bring that potential to life. You will stretch your capacity to hold both a "big-picture view" and many details at the same time. You will learn skills and tools for finding clarity within confusion, for inspiring creativity and innovation within stuck or mired situations, and for discovering the next action steps for forward movement. You will develop skills and tools for reducing stress and increasing resilience in the face of uncertainty, hardship, and challenge. And you will expand your capacities for deep listening and awareness—hearing what is beneath the words and observing what is beneath the surface of complex circumstances and situations.

Just as Transformational Presence is built on a way of being, a skill set, and an approach, an intentional culture is also created by a common set of practices and approaches, as well as a way of being together. The more a group, team, system, or organization adopts and practices the Transformational Presence approaches, the more open, intuitive, creative, resourceful, resilient, impactful, and expansive the culture can become.

Gerhard, the CEO of a global technology services company, says, "So much has happened for me and for our company since we were first introduced to the Transformational Presence work. Most of our top leadership team has now been through a Transformational Presence development program, and we all acknowledge that decision-making, both day-to-day and long-term, is much easier and clearer now. As the CEO, I can honestly say that my grounding in Transformational Presence is never far away. As a leadership team, we can still get caught up on emotional rollercoasters from time to time. Yet we've recognized that when this happens, it's usually because we need to let go of an old way of doing something and move forward in a new and sometimes scary way. Yet even when the rollercoaster appears, we recognize that we now have tools and frameworks that help us get grounded again, find clarity, and take new action. And as a team, we're getting better and better at recognizing the rollercoaster before it sweeps us away."

Barbara shares a story of the difference Transformational Presence is making in her leadership work in healthcare. She had designed a lifestyle program for people challenged with Multiple Sclerosis. The program was based on new research and her own experience in supporting patients. However, the partnering company for the program was very stuck in an old paradigm of treatment for this condition.

A big conflict emerged between those who were supporting Barbara's new lifestyle program and those supporting the old-school approaches from the partner company. However, Barbara chose to remain present and open. She listened beneath the words and sensed where energy was moving and where it was stuck. She asked questions from an open and compassionate place, sensing the fears and hesitations that were not being given a voice. She chose to work *with* the resistance in the room rather than fight against it or try to change it. This allowed some of the deeper issues to come to the surface.

Within a very short time, the tone of the conversation had changed significantly and the two sides were beginning to find their way together. In the end, the partner company was willing to try the new lifestyle program with some of their patients and see what would happen. The end result was great success for those patients, and soon the new lifestyle program became the accepted course of treatment in that particular center.

Transformational Presence involves both developing skills and expanding capacities. Skills are things you learn how to do. To be skilled at something means that you can do it well. Capacity has to do with your ability to receive or contain. Within our context, we're speaking of capacity as your ability to receive and hold information, and to create or hold a space for all that is happening. In today's world, we need greater capacities for sensing many layers of awareness, for embracing many levels of experience and emotion, for taking in and processing enormous amounts of information, and for being present with many layers of complexity.

We build and expand those capacities by developing and honing our Transformational Presence skills. The Transformational Presence approach offers simple yet powerful skills and tools that cut to the essence of what is happening, bringing clarity, insight, and awareness. As we practice those skills, they stretch our capacity for recognizing and making sense of the many layers of complexity in situations and circumstances, as well as many layers of emotion and experience. We expand our capacities for seeing and sensing many pieces of the puzzle, how they are moving or are stuck in relationship to one another, and how everything fits together.

The concepts, tools, models, and approaches we explore both in this book and in the companion *Tools, Skills, and Frameworks* book will help you to build your Transformational Presence skill set. Those skills will support you in creating cultures and environments that encourage breakthrough, transformation, effective action, and lasting success. What you learn here will help you be better prepared for meeting whatever each day brings, for understanding what is happening from multiple perspectives, for navigating the unknown, and helping those around you to do the same.

Transformational Presence is a leadership, coaching, and service approach whose time has come—a way of living, leading, and serving that can make a difference and help us create a world that works.

CHAPTER 2

The Great Breaking Open

For a seed to achieve its greatest expression, it must come completely undone.
The shell cracks, its insides come out and everything changes. To someone
who doesn't understand growth, it would look like complete destruction.

—Cynthia Occelli, author and blogger

Life does not accommodate you; it shatters you.
Every seed destroys its container or else there would be no fruition.

—Florida Scott-Maxwell, poet, playwright, and author

WE'RE LIVING IN A WORLD where it seems that every major system and structure is coming completely undone. The shells are cracking, the insides are coming out, and everything is changing. It looks and feels as though much of the world as we have known it is breaking down, falling apart, or being destroyed.

Yet I see this as a time of the Great Breaking Open. Challenging, difficult, and even painful as it might be, this is how growth and evolution work. Part of what makes it challenging and difficult is our *resistance* to the growth and evolution process. Looking at what is happening through the lens of the Great Breaking Open invites new perspectives and possibilities.

Change is happening at unprecedented rates. Everything is in transition. Yet when things are in transition, energy is moving and there are opportunities for transformation. Transformation is much easier when things are shifting anyway. Disruption is already happening, people are stirred up, and they're more willing to try a different approach. Transformation is much harder when things are rigid and fixed. The breaking open that is happening right before our eyes and under our feet is actually creating conditions, situations, and circumstances that are ripe for transformation. It's up to us to be clear and intentional about how we respond to what is happening.

The Great Breaking Open is cutting through to the core of our societal structures and to the core of our being as individuals. For as long as many of us can remember, our societies, governments, businesses, and education systems have increasingly focused on short-term, bottom-line results. As problems have arisen, we have increasingly tended to address only the surface issues, looked for quick fixes, and opted for the most attractive immediate result. As a result, we have increasingly neglected to pay attention to the pressures that have been building under the surface because important core issues have not been addressed. Unfortunately, this has been at the expense of our future and our societal wellbeing.

The Great Breaking Open is now forcing us to look at these core issues. And these core issues need more than just "fixes." Instead, they require new forms, new structures, new approaches, and new policies. And that will require us to create new ways of living and working together.

After the end of the Cold War, the U.S. Army War College described the world as volatile, uncertain, complex, and ambiguous. The acronym VUCA, created from those four descriptive words, first appeared in the late 1990s. After the terrorist attacks of September 11, 2001, the term was adopted by the business world to describe the turbulence, chaos, and rapid change that has since become the "new normal"—political, economic, and social unrest; terrorist attacks; government structures coming undone. None of these things exist in isolation. They are all somehow connected and part of a much larger story—the ongoing story of human and social development and evolution.

On the surface, it's a VUCA world. Yet there's a seismic shift going on underneath the breaking open of systems, structures, and societies—it's the *breaking open of the human spirit.* I believe that, if we pay attention, it is this deeper breaking open of the human spirit that holds the power for our future. I am confident that if we focus beyond the struggle and upheaval, we will find a bigger vision of our world that has been waiting for us for some time. The Great Breaking Open seems to be telling us that the human spirit has grown impatient and a bigger vision is now required. The time for movement and action is now.

The breaking open of the human spirit is not a comfortable place to be. And what makes it particularly uncomfortable is that we are not just witnessing it; we are *experiencing* it. All of us. Granted, some are on the front lines more than others. However, everyone is touched in some way. The breaking open is just manifesting in different ways for different people.

Many people are experiencing the breaking open of their fundamental survival spirit, driven by their basic human need to be shown dignity and respect. Think of the hundreds of thousands of refugees who have fled their home countries and risked their lives and their children's lives for the chance for something better. Think of all the people who have endured repression or prejudice due to the color of their skin, their gender identification, or their ethnic or economic background, and who long to be accepted as equal members of society.

Others are experiencing the breaking open of suppressed rage, pain, resentment, and fear that can no longer be contained. As their rage and pain explodes, the result can manifest as violence or fanaticism. They have not felt seen, respected, or valued. They believe that they are being cheated by systems designed to "keep them in their place." And there is evidence that, in many cases, they're right.

Yet others are feeling their hearts breaking open to the awareness that everyone and everything is interconnected. They can no longer separate themselves from the pain and suffering of others. Increasingly, their compassion is moving them into service. Whole communities have responded to the refugees with enormous outpourings of support. People have opened their homes to strangers from far-away lands and sponsored refugee families. People from all over the world have traveled at their own expense to provide aid in war-torn regions or places that have experienced catastrophes. Others have been deeply involved in peaceful social action movements or have regularly volunteered their help in soup kitchens, homeless shelters, and other service agencies.

It's not the first time that this has happened, and it won't be the last. Yet it's critical that we pay attention to this breaking open now, both within our own circles and beyond.

The human spirit is stronger, more powerful, and more resilient than many of us have ever imagined. It's much bigger than any national spirit or the spirit of any political party, religion, or economic class. The human spirit has no economic, political, or religious affiliation. It has a *human* affiliation. And it has a strong sense of its place within a more-than-human world.

The human spirit is breaking open to show us in no uncertain terms that we have been dreaming too small a dream, holding too small a vision. As our view of the future has gotten increasingly shorter over the last decades, our collective dreams of what could be possible have gotten smaller. It's been more than fifty years since the Reverend Dr. Martin Luther King inspired the world with his "I have a dream" speech at the 1963 March on Washington—more than fifty years since President John F. Kennedy challenged the United States of America to go to the moon. The next iteration of our world is waiting to be born. It's time for a bigger dream.

At the same time, there is a great backlash and outcry from those who are attached to a particular belief system, a way of life that is no longer in sync with a rapidly evolving society and consciousness, and those who are feeling left behind, whether socially, economically, or spiritually. This is all a part of the Great Breaking Open of the human spirit.

When the dam holding back feelings and emotions in the human consciousness breaks open, the full spectrum of response comes flooding out. The full spectrum of human experiences and emotions is so much wider than many of us can wrap our heads around. Intellectually, it's difficult to comprehend the depth and breadth of what some of our fellow human beings are experiencing. Nor can we intellectually understand the actions that some of our fellow human beings take, or the massive system breakdowns that are happening everywhere. In our efforts to put what is happening into a simpler context that we can understand, we just put a label on it, such as calling it a "VUCA world."

Yet while our intellectual minds are easily overwhelmed by all that is happening, our *hearts* actually have the capacity to take it all in. And herein lies the fundamental shift that is trying to happen through the Great Breaking Open. If we are willing to step beyond the intellect's fears, anger, doubts, and discomfort, even for just a few moments, and focus our attention on the awareness, understanding, and wisdom of the heart, something changes in our perception of where we are and what is happening.

The human heart has an uncanny ability to embrace the full spectrum of what is happening without judgment, and, somehow, to begin making sense of it. Somewhere from within our greater knowing, a new level of understanding begins to emerge.

It's also critical that we find language to talk about these concepts that doesn't limit them. Some people would label them as "spiritual" concepts. Yet the term "spiritual" has different connotations for different people.

In the broadest terms, we're talking about *energy* technology—more specifically, the *human energy and awareness* technology. We're talking about different aspects of human intelligence—head and heart, intellect and intuition, ego and soul. We're talking about a technology of life that can help us understand *everything*—situations, circumstances, relationships, business, society, government, education, healthcare—as energy in motion.

It may seem odd to use the word "technology" in this context. Yet in its root meaning, the word "technology" comes from two ancient Greek words: *techne* and *logia*. *Techne* literally means an art, skill, craft, or technique. *Logia* refers to a collection of techniques, skills, methods, and processes used in the accomplishment of a particular objective. "Technology" is the application of tools and methods—a way of applying tools and knowledge. In Transformational Presence, we apply the human energy technology first to understand how life works as energy in motion. Then we apply that understanding to help us create a healthy and thriving world—a world that works.

In the human energy technology, the intellect is the primary mind of the ego. It resides in the head and is centered in the brain. The intellect's fundamental job is to make sure that we're OK—to ensure our survival. Therefore, its instinctual response to anything that happens to us and around us is to manage and control everything in order to keep us safe.

The intellect attempts to put experiences and information into boxes, categories, and contexts that it already understands. It wants to make sense of everything that happens as quickly as possible so that it can analyze those situations for safety and security. The intellect wants to fix, to solve, and to alleviate our immediate pain and discomfort.

In times of challenge or crisis, the intellect will tend to put its own perceived needs and desires ahead of anyone else's. This is not a judgment on the intellect. It's simply doing its job, which is to protect your interests.

This is the intellect's *techne* and *logia*—the technology of the intellect. And that intellect technology is just one part of the larger human energy technology. Therefore, it's important that we allow the intellect to do its job, while, at the same time, remain aware that we are more than intellect alone.

The intelligence of the heart, on the other hand, is the mind of the soul. It has the capacity to see the big picture—to take in all that is happening, understand how it all fits together, and show us a path forward. Since 1991, the Institute of HeartMath (heartmath.org) in Boulder Creek, California, has done extensive research on the intelligence of the heart, the intuitive mind, and heart-brain coherence. According to their research, the heart's electromagnetic field is approximately five thousand times greater than the electromagnetic field of the brain (Childre, Martin, and Beech, p. 33). This says to me that the heart's field of awareness and influence is five thousand times greater than that of the brain or intellect. Doc Childre, the founder of the Institute, says, "The heart isn't only *open* to new possibilities, it actively scans for them, ever seeking new, intuitive understanding. Ultimately, the head 'knows' but the heart 'understands.' The heart operates in a more refined range of information-processing capability, and it has a strong influence over how our brain functions." (Childre, Martin, and Beech, p. 6)

As a society, we're not very practiced at acknowledging the deep feelings of the heart and letting the heart show us the way forward. We're not very practiced at being with uncomfortable emotions and experiences. Instead, we tend to become quickly overwhelmed by our feelings and run to the head (where it feels safer!) to "figure out" how to deal with these feelings and what we should do next.

As a result, two things happen.

First, we don't give the heart a chance to do what it's really good at—to intuit the bigger picture and bring us clarity and understanding.

Second, we create a split within ourselves, both individually and collectively, further separating head from heart. That separation creates an increasingly wider gap between intellect and intuition, between ego and soul. We keep breaking apart the partnerships within us that are essential to the full functioning of the human energy technology.

As that split grows wider, we increase the odds that, at some point, we will crack open in search of our own wholeness and greater potential, just as the seed must crack open in order to grow. Our innate potential, individually as well as collectively as societies and organizational systems, is a powerful force that wants to be fully expressed and come into form. It's driven by the evolutionary force or intelligence that we spoke about in the Introduction. If we don't acknowledge that potential and create the best possible conditions for it to come into form, it will eventually burst open out of its desire to be fully expressed. To return to the seed analogy from the quotes that opened this chapter, the increasing pressure within the seed for life and forward evolution can ultimately become too great, and the seed can explode.

This is what we see happening today. The floodgates holding back human potential, experience, and emotion are breaking open. The wider the split gets between head and heart in our society, the more we will witness circumstances and events such as we have now. Instead of creating stability and safety, we will continue creating a VUCA world.

The heart is well attuned to recognize and acknowledge the human spirit. It is also fully attuned to the emerging greater potentials, both within us as individuals as well as within our relationships, systems, organizations, projects, and visions. At the same time, the heart has an enormous innate capacity for embracing the full spectrum of thoughts, feelings, and emotions, as well as the big picture of circumstances and situations. It has the capacity to accept everything simply as information, without judging it as good or bad, right or wrong. The heart integrates that information into our awareness and communicates its new understanding to the intellect. The intellect can then organize that information and store it in its extraordinary filing system so that we can access it on demand.

At first, we may experience this communication only as an "inner knowing or sensing." The intellect may not be able to describe the experience in words right away. However, if we will just be patient, stay connected to the heart, and give ourselves a little time, the intellect will begin to find words to express our new perspective and understanding.

Our VUCA world presents us with unprecedented challenges. Yet if we drop underneath those challenges, we also find enormous opportunities. One of the ancient wisdom teachings that can help us better understand how the world works is the Principle of Polarity. This principle tells us that nothing can exist without the possibility of its opposite also being present. Therefore, a challenge cannot exist unless there is also potential for creating something new. This is why I refer to what is happening today as the Great Breaking Open instead of the "great breaking down."

It's time for a shift in our fundamental approach to life. At the mass consciousness level, we're conditioned to engage with life first from the head and only occasionally engage the heart to soften the edges. It's time to turn that around.

It's time to engage first from the heart to gather information and see the big picture, and then bring in the intellect to do what it does best—to organize, strategize, and move into effective action based on the big-picture view of the heart. This is, in essence, the foundational skill set upon which Transformational Presence is built.

However, we need ways to talk about this that people can understand and immediately begin to apply in their everyday lives and work. To just say, "You have to open your heart!" can be perceived by many people as overly simplistic, naïve, and disconnected from reality. It can be interpreted as a feel-good-warm-and-fuzzy approach that has no substance. And it can give the impression that you are in denial of the magnitude of what is happening.

This is completely understandable, because in the mass consciousness, we are only just beginning to grasp the enormous power of the heart intelligence and all that is available to us through the greater human energy technology. For many people, this is still completely new territory.

If we want to navigate our way through this VUCA world rather than be trapped by it, we need tools and skills for accessing the power of the heart and for transforming awareness, perception, and understanding. And that's what Transformational Presence offers. Again, Transformational Presence is a skill set—a set of skills and tools that builds inner capacities for perception, awareness, understanding, navigating complexity, and taking effective and sustainable action. Transformational Presence offers *techne*—art, skill, craft, and technique—and *logia*—a collection of tools, methods, approaches, and processes. Transformational Presence is actually a new leadership and life awareness technology.

Nobel Prize winning physicist Max Planck said, "When you change the way you look at things, the things you look at change." Our job in Transformational Presence is not to change *what* people think—it's to open up *how* they think by giving them tools and skills that transform their understanding, awareness, and perception, and ultimately expand their worldview.

The fundamental change we can make in *how* people think, starting today, is to engage the awareness and intelligence that is rooted in the heart. As the heart shows us a bigger picture, our perception and understanding of what is happening expands. And as our perception and understanding expand, we begin to sense our next steps. Heart and head then partner to create a strategy and move into action. The human energy technology system can now kick in, and we have a much better chance of creating a more whole, equitable, and sustainable future.

The Great Breaking Open has brought us to a powerful moment of choice: Will we continue to push down the collective human spirit in service of protecting our own personal, family, business, or national interests? Or will we lift up the collective human spirit and focus our attention now on creating a world in which everyone has the possibility to provide for themselves, their families, and their communities? Will we create a world that works for all or just for a select few?

We are faced with these choices every day on every level of society, from the personal to the global. It's critical that we pay attention to what is happening on every level. Another one of the ancient wisdom teachings, the Principle of Correspondence, says, "As above, so below; as below, so above." The fundamental energy behind whatever is happening in the bigger world is also manifesting in some way in your personal world. At the same time, the energy behind whatever is happening in your personal world is manifesting in some way in the larger world. Just as many things are breaking open in the systems and structures of society, education, healthcare, business, and government, things are also breaking open in our personal lives. Relationships, family structures, and friendships break open. Emotions and feelings break open within us. The stories or circumstances may be different on the outside, yet at the most basic levels, it's all about things breaking open.

The Great Breaking Open is asking us to stretch our perception, our beliefs, and our worldviews. It's asking us to push beyond the boundaries of our imaginations and begin to sense the new world that we could create. Something more wants to happen. The Great Breaking Open is asking us to dream a bigger dream—to create a bigger vision of who we can be and what we can do, both as individuals and as societies. It's asking us to create that new world.

No one person can see or sense that bigger vision alone. Yet together, we can tap into that bigger dream and then bring it into reality. The very act of dreaming together and *responding* to the dream will itself be the beginning of the healing process—the return to wholeness—for the human spirit.

This takes us back to Ari Wallach's Longpath and his three transformative ways of thinking that we discussed in the Introduction. We may not see the full healing of the human spirit and of our societies in our lifetimes. It's taken us many generations to get to where we are now; transformation will also take time. That's OK. Transformation happens through process, not through outcomes.

Through our step-by-step process together, we can discover a new level of wholeness within ourselves. And in turn, we can create a new level of wholeness within our world.

The Great Breaking Open continues all around us and within us. The human spirit has broken open. There is no turning back. What comes next is up to us.

CHAPTER 3

We Start With Just Three Questions

Do what you can with what you have where you are.

—Theodore Roosevelt

THESE WORDS FROM THEODORE ROOSEVELT offer practical advice for challenging times. Something about that statement grabbed my attention the first time that I read it. However, as I kept sitting with Roosevelt's words, I began to realize that in today's world, we might be better served by turning his statement around, starting with the last part first: Where you are, with what you have, do what you can.

When we are in the throes of a "breaking open," it can be hard to know where we are and what is happening. When the ground beneath our feet is shifting and everything around us seems to be changing, we may even feel like we no longer recognize the world around us. So a first step is to find some clarity about *where we are* now and "what wants to happen" next.

The question, "What wants to happen?" acknowledges that there is probably a message to be sensed or heard, a shift waiting to occur, a door that is opening, or an opportunity waiting for us to notice—something that "wants to happen." Getting clear about *where we are* includes peering into the present circumstance to discover the seed of potential or the seed of the future (they're often the same thing) that is waiting to emerge. We then become stewards for that potential, supporting the unfolding of "what wants to happen."

This is actually what being a visionary is all about. It's not so much about seeing what will happen in the future. The true visionary peers deep into the present moment to discover the greatest seed of the future that is now ready to burst open. And then the visionary begins to nurture that seed.

"What wants to happen" is not necessarily the same as what *you* want to happen. "What wants to happen?" is a question in service of something bigger than you—sometimes much bigger. "What wants to happen?" is in service of a common good. It's got to work for everyone. While everyone may not get all of what they need or want, the idea is that everyone gets at least some. And basic needs are met for all.

The middle part of Roosevelt's statement—*with what you have*—can also be confusing when everything is changing. It's easy to get so caught up in what *we no longer have* or what is slipping away that often we don't recognize what *we actually do have.*

So the second step is to recognize the resources that we have within us as well as the resources around us that we can access right where we are, right now. Most of the time, there are more resources available to us than we first realize.

Which takes us back to the first part of Roosevelt's statement—*do what you can.* Part of what makes a "breaking open" so challenging is our conditioning to go straight away to the intellect and ask, "What can we do to fix this?" That's a very difficult question to answer when we don't have a clear sense of where we are and what we have.

Therefore, we start with the last part of Roosevelt's advice first. If we pause to gain some clarity about *where we are* and *what we have*, then *what we can do* will start to reveal itself. And as *what we can do* starts to become clear, we're able to take our first steps into action.

The Transformational Presence approach is built on just three simple yet powerful questions:

1. What wants to happen?

2. Who is that asking me to be?

3. What is that asking me to do?

We've already talked about the bigger meaning of the first question, "What wants to happen?" Other ways of asking this question could be: What is the opportunity available to us right now? What is the breakthrough that is waiting to happen? What is the shift that is trying to happen? What is this situation or circumstance trying to tell us? If what is happening is trying to give us a message to help us go forward, what is that message?

The second question speaks to who we are—to our personal presence. It's about how we "show up" and the personal qualities and characteristics that we can bring to our leadership and service. Perhaps "what wants to happen" is asking you to be courageous, truthful, playful, or creative. Or perhaps it's asking you to take on a particular role. Who is it asking you to be?

Notice that the question is not, "Who do you *want* to be?" The question is, "Who is 'what wants to happen' *asking* you to be?" Your head may be confused by that question, but your heart will understand. Your heart can tune into what is happening and sense or intuit who the circumstance needs for you to be in order to move things forward. The key is to let "what wants to happen" be your guide. It will tell you what it needs. You don't have to "figure it out." The message is more likely to come from your heart than from your head.

Then the third question is the call to action. Again, the question is not asking you to figure out what to do next. Instead, the question is inviting you to let "what wants to happen" show you what it needs from you in order for the greatest possible outcome to unfold.

These three simple yet powerful questions cut to the essence of what is happening and what is being asked for. Don't worry about having the full picture right away. Just start with what you are able to sense and understand from these three questions right now. And then take a step. Be who you are asked to be and do what you are asked to do. Then come back to the first question again.

In essence, the Transformational Presence approach is to ask these three questions, respond by taking a step in action, ask the three questions again, take your next step, and continue this process for as long as is needed.

The approach can be simplified even more through this model:

Opportunity ➜ *Presence* ➜ *Action*

Answering the first question establishes the potential that is waiting to emerge. Answering the second question establishes who you need to be—what parts of you need to show up or be developed in order for you to be a steward for that potential. In other words, it establishes your presence. Then answering the third question clarifies the next action step to be taken.

The key is to ask these three questions in this order. When faced with a challenge or opportunity, most of us have been conditioned to go straight to question #3. Actually, as in Roosevelt's statement, we don't really even ask *that* question. Instead, we ask, "What are we going to do?" or "What is our plan of action?" We go straight into figure-it-out-and-get-it-done mode without realizing that there could actually be some important information hidden within what is going on.

There is always something that "wants to happen." So we begin with stepping back for a moment, using our heart intelligence to tap into that hidden (or not so hidden!) potential, and listening—paying attention to it with all of our inner and outer senses.

As we begin to sense what wants to happen, that potential will start to show us who we need to be in order to turn that potential into reality. It will tell us what parts of ourselves—what inner qualities—are needed to bring this potential into form. As we start to become that person or embody those qualities, we begin to recognize the next step to be taken.

These three questions are the foundation of my approach to everything. Whether I am writing an article or blog post, preparing a workshop or keynote lecture, addressing a challenge or obstacle, or visioning the next big steps for the Center for Transformational Presence, my first question is some variation of "What wants to happen?" For example:

What is the core message that wants to come through this article? What is the greatest need that this workshop should address for the participants? What message is the obstacle I am facing trying to tell me—what am I not yet seeing? What is the next great calling in our work at the Center? What is the potential that is trying to get our attention? I take time to listen, sense, and feel.

Then I ask that potential how it needs for me to show up. Who does it need for me to be to help it manifest? What is important about my personal presence in this situation? What qualities must I bring to the moment?

And then I ask the potential to show me what to do. Sometimes, I only sense a next step; at other times, I can begin to see the whole path ahead of me—who to talk to, what resources to gather, and even the step-by-step strategy. I've learned to trust that, if I pay attention, I will find what I need to move forward.

The whole process is very fluid. These three simple yet powerful questions are always playing the background of my awareness.

In the *Tools, Skills, and Frameworks* book, you will find many practical frameworks, tools, and applications to help you access your heart intelligence and quickly find the answers to these three questions. However, as you may have already discovered, simply asking these three questions in that order can already shift your focus to your heart so that the exploration begins there rather than in your head. The simplicity of the Transformational Presence approach tends to take you straight to the heart intelligence where you can continue to expand your capacities for awareness and discovery, perception and understanding, clarity and action.

The Three Questions can then become a powerful guiding light—a light that will illuminate your path forward, help you become the person, team, or organization you need to be for whatever opportunity or challenge is in front of you, and show you the next steps to take.

These three deep and simple questions can become the foundation of your life and work and the foundation of how a team or organization approaches their work, mission, and vision. They offer an alternative to the big question of "How can I/we do it?" In fact, as your ability to sense what wants to happen gets stronger and stronger, the question, "How?" will come up less and less. Instead of asking, "How?" you ask, "What is my next step?" The Three Questions offer a pathway towards making the difference you are here to make.

CHAPTER 4

How the World Works—
Three Basic Principles

If you want to find the secrets of the universe,
think in terms of energy, frequency, and vibration.

—Nikola Tesla
Serbian-American inventor, engineer, physicist, and futurist

ON THE SURFACE, IT APPEARS that we live in a three-dimensional world of form. Some forms appear to be solid and tangible—a tree, a person, a house. Others seem less tangible—a situation, a relationship, a family, a company or organization, a country, and even our world.

Some of the less tangible forms have physical representations—a company has an office building, a country has a certain amount of land within marked borders. Yet what actually makes up a family, a partnership, a situation, a company, a country, and even the world, are the qualities, beliefs, worldviews, relationships, practices, traditions, instincts, lifestyles, and interdependence of its inhabitants—both human and non-human. From quantum physics, we understand that each of those forms, whether tangible or intangible, is, at the most fundamental level, made up of energy that is vibrating to a particular frequency and organized in a particular pattern.

Quantum physics helps us understand that everything, at its most fundamental level, is made up of vibrating packets of energy. In other words, fundamentally, everything is energy. Energy in its pure form is neutral. It's not good or bad, right or wrong, positive or negative. What gives energy a particular quality is how we engage with it and how we use it.

Furthermore, quantum physics shows us that energy can organize itself into a fixed, three-dimensional form (in quantum physics language, this is referred to as "particle" form), or it can take a fluid form (known in quantum physics as "wave" form). When packets of energy become "particles," they take on specific forms and occupy specific spaces and times. A chair in your living room is in "particle" form, as is your desk, an apple, a tree, or an animal or person.

Yet at the same time, all of these things simultaneously exist in "wave" form. In the quantum reality, they also exist as waves of energy—as ideas or concepts—vibrating over a larger space-time continuum and taking no specific form. So, at the most fundamental level, the chair, desk, apple, tree, animal, or person are also energy in motion.

The idea that energy can behave like both waves and particles at the same time is known in quantum physics as the Wave-Particle Theory. You might think of "wave" as pure potential without specific form and without specific time-space location. "Particle," on the other hand, is created when the wave "collapses" into a specific form and space-time location. The *idea* of a chair is in wave form; once someone takes that idea and builds a chair in three-dimensional, physical reality, the chair is now also in particle form. The chair is both an idea (wave) and an object in physical reality (particle) at the same time.

The Participant-Observer Principle, also from quantum physics, tells us that our presence and interaction with the wave has an influence on the kind of particle that the wave will collapse into. In other words, energy takes particular forms based on the presence, choices, behaviors, attitudes, and actions of the participants.

For example, two people may have exactly the same idea for an invention, yet how they actually create that invention in form will be different. Their particular circumstances, perspectives, desires, and needs will all influence how and what they create.

In the same way, if two teams are given exactly the same problem to solve, they will fulfill their assignment in different ways. Because the two teams are made up of different people, there will be differences in how they perceive the problem and, therefore, in how they choose to approach it. The outcomes will be determined by the personalities, approaches, perceptions, understanding, engagements, and culture of the two different teams.

(If these principles are new to you, Chapters 12 – 15 of my book *Create A World That Works* offer simple and understandable explanations of these and other fundamental quantum physics principles.)

A situation is also energy in motion—the energy is organizing and manifesting itself in a particular way. Out of the "wave" of many possibilities, the thoughts, feelings, and perceptions of all of the people, along with the various conditions involved, have converged to create the circumstance of the moment.

The "form" of the circumstance or situation is a representation of the energy within it. When we try to "fix" the situation, we are trying to change the form. Changing the form of what is happening can be hard work, especially when a particular momentum has gathered steam. However, when we go to the underlying energy (wave) and make a shift in the energy first, the situation will start to change as a result.

For example, when a project in an organization is not coming together quickly enough, the first reaction is often to ask, "How can we fix it?" Or, "How can we speed up the process? What do we need to do differently?"

Sometimes, resolving the issue can be as simple as that. However, often the "problem" is a symptom of a deeper issue—the energy within the form. Perhaps this is actually not the right project at this time. Maybe there is a lack of alignment between the values and passions of the team members and what they are being asked to do. Or perhaps there is a lack of trust, support, and respect within the culture of the organization that is undermining everything.

Form follows energy. Therefore, *the fastest and most effective way to make a lasting change in the form of something is to start by transforming the energy that makes up that form.* The first step in transforming a relationship, team, or project is to transform the fundamental perceptions, ideals, beliefs, attitudes, desires, interests, and even visions that make up its foundation. In other words, our job is to transform the energy to the degree that it begins creating new patterns of behavior, choices, and actions. Otherwise, even though we make adjustments or changes in form, the old energy patterns are still in place. The energy has not transformed, so the changes in form are not likely to last. This is true, whether in our personal lives, a family, a company or organization, an institution, or a society.

The Transformational Presence approach is rooted in three fundamental principles that are built on the understanding that, fundamentally, everything is energy. These principles were the foundation of ancient wisdom teachings about how the world works, and now quantum physics gives us the science behind these ancient principles. We refer to them as the Three Fundamental Principles.

Principle #1—Everything is energy in motion, a part of a larger process unfolding. Form follows energy. Nothing exists in isolation. The more we understand situations within their larger contexts, the more easily we can understand the bigger picture of what is happening and can find our next steps forward. The form that a situation takes at any particular time is a manifestation of the energy within the situation at that time.

Principle #2—Energy cannot be created or destroyed; it can only be transformed. Whatever is in front of us, at least for this moment, is what is available to us to work with right now. It's our next creative partner. It may not be our only creative partner, but it is one of them. We may not like what is in front of us, but it is what is there at the moment. Finding a way to *work with* what is in front of us instead of push or fight against it is almost always easier and more productive. The same is true for feelings and emotions. They are also energy. We can't get rid of them, but we can transform them.

Principle #3—The world is built on a matrix of relationships. Relationships are not just between people—there are also relationships between people and ideas, people and beliefs, people and circumstances, people and their environment, as well as relationships between ideas, beliefs, and circumstances themselves. The most effective space for transformational work is almost always in the relationship space—the space *in between* people, ideas, beliefs, circumstances, and aspects or components of their environment.

Let's explore each of these principles more deeply.

PRINCIPLE #1—Everything is energy in motion, a part of a larger process unfolding. Form follows energy.

Part of the challenge in navigating our current VUCA world is that we tend to view situations, events, and circumstances as separate and unrelated to each other. In the Transformational Presence approach, we start from the premise that whatever is happening is not an isolated event, but rather is a part of a much larger process unfolding. We begin by looking first at the big picture in order to better understand the detail of what is happening right now.

This first principle reminds us that everything—every project, situation, circumstance, relationship, and even feeling and emotion—is, at the most fundamental level, vibrating energy. At any moment in time, the vibrational frequency and pattern of that energy is manifesting in a particular form. As much as it may look or feel like that form is permanent, it is not. It is simply the form that the energy is taking in that moment. There have been other events and circumstances leading up to this moment; what is happening now, as well as the choices and actions taken, will lead to other circumstances or events.

Therefore, our circumstance or situation is a manifestation of the energy as it exists right now. Because energy is in constant motion, it is also constantly changing and shifting. When the energy shifts, the form will also change in some way. Therefore, by the laws of nature, any situation or circumstance will continue evolving and changing. The ways in which we engage with our circumstances and situations influences how they shift, change, and evolve, and the pace at which those shifts happen. Again, the Participant-Observer Principle.

It's easy to get caught up in viewing what is happening in our lives or the projects we're working on as isolated events, forgetting that they are related to other events in other moments of time. Too often, we don't "connect the dots," recognizing how what is happening fits together with things that happened or choices that we made in the past, or how our current situation relates to parallel situations around us or in the world. Life doesn't always unfold in a linear pattern or flow.

The more we understand this principle and work with the events and circumstances of our lives as energy in motion and as part of a larger process, the easier everything becomes. Especially when faced with challenge and difficulty, it can be helpful to remember that whatever is happening is just what is happening right now. Nothing is permanent. Everything is energy in flow—everything is a part of a larger process that is unfolding.

In the companion *Tools, Skills, and Frameworks* book, you will find an exercise to help you experience time as energy in motion and see your present circumstances within a much larger context.

PRINCIPLE #2—Energy cannot be created or destroyed; it can only be transformed.

The second principle tells us that, much as we might like to, at the energy level, we can't get rid of something we don't like—a thought, a feeling, a belief, a circumstance, or a situation. The good news, however, is that we can transform it.

One of the tenets of Transformational Presence work is:

A problem is not something to be solved;
it's a message to be listened to.

Our job is to listen to the message, discover the greater potential wanting to unfold, and partner with that potential to create a new reality.

Partnering with "what is" instead of fighting against it is the first step into the "flow" of what wants to happen. We tap into a greater potential wanting to be realized and partner with that potential for new creation. Not only do things get easier, but often we also discover greater possibilities than we had imagined before.

If you've ever participated in acting or musical improvisation, you know that the primary rule is that you must accept and work with whatever your improvisation partners give you. If you don't, there is a good chance that the whole performance will fall apart. Improvisation is a co-creative process. You work with your partners and with whatever is available in the moment to co-create something new together.

Life works pretty much the same way. It's an ongoing improvisation—a co-creative process with the people, ideas, beliefs, and circumstances around us. When we accept whatever comes to us and *work with it* instead of push against it, things are a lot easier. We step beyond our judgments and opinions, likes and dislikes, and accept that, at least for the moment, whatever is in front of us is what we have to work with. It may not be the only thing we have to work with, but it is what is in front of us at the moment. Whether or not we like it, approve of it, or care about it doesn't matter. It's what is here. When we are willing to co-create with what presents itself rather than resist it, there is a much better chance that something new can emerge.

This "push against or flow with" concept is also one of the fundamental principles in martial arts. The idea is to take your opponent's energy and *work with it* instead of fight against it—to receive your opponent's energy and let it move *through* you, transmuting that energy into your own strength and power. If you push against your opponent, you actually give your power away and become weaker.

The same is true with something we consider to be a problem. When we push against it, we give it more power. We lose our energy to the problem. However, in the Transformational Presence approach, we understand that a problem is not something to be solved (push against); it is a message to be listened to (flow with). Within this context, co-creation is a process of intuiting the message that the challenge is trying to show us, tapping into the potential that is waiting to emerge, and *flowing with* that potential. The potential itself becomes our co-creative partner.

It's important to note that "flow with" is not the same thing as "go with the flow!" "Go with the flow" means just going along with what is currently happening. However, what is happening may not be leading the situation in a direction that serves the greatest potential. If you are working through a personal situation, sometimes it feels easier to give in to your habits or patterns of response and let whatever happens happen. If it is a group or organizational issue, the pull to follow the group reaction or a path of perceived safety, security, comfort, or familiarity may be very strong. These are examples of "going with the flow."

Yet as you sense the greater potential waiting to unfold, you may recognize that *what is happening now* and what truly *wants to happen* in service of something bigger are two different things. Intuiting the hidden message and potential is what makes "flow with" different from just giving up or giving in to how the situation is currently unfolding.

As an example, perhaps you have experienced a time when you or your team has committed to a project or goal. However, from the beginning, something about the project wasn't working. Intuitively, you knew that all of the signals were pointing to a significant shift that wanted to happen in both the company culture as well as some of their fundamental business practices. Perhaps you weren't the only one who sensed this. However, speaking out could have been risky. Therefore, you and others chose to just "go with the flow"—to follow the ingrained patterns of the organization, and not rock the boat. What happened as a result?

In the end, not following the signals of what wants to happen usually leads to more frustration, cynicism, and disengagement. Furthermore, the project is not likely to succeed.

"Flow with," on the other hand, could mean listening more deeply to what wants to happen, and using the Three Fundamental Questions to find your next step. "Flow with" may require speaking out, taking action, or challenging the system. Yet if the system is open enough to be willing to listen and consider another possibility, the potential can lead you forward into new ways of engaging, new practices, and ultimately a healthier, happier, more aligned, and more productive organizational culture.

The potential that is trying to emerge needs a partner or a steward to help it manifest within the current circumstance. It is up to us to be that steward—to co-create with the potential by saying "Yes" to what it asks us for. "Flow with" is a pro-active process of sensing the greatest potential waiting to unfold in service of all involved and then doing our part to steward that potential into reality.

This second principle invites us to consider that the reason a challenge or problem exists is to help us discover something else that is waiting to emerge. It invites us to view the challenge as a gift or as a message bearer, not as something to get rid of.

Because this "Push Against – Flow With" concept is so foundational to Transformational Presence, let's do a little mini-coaching session to help you ground this concept in your understanding. You can also find a short video to lead you through this mini-coaching session at TransformationalPresenceBook.com.

Bring to your awareness something in either your professional or personal life that you view as a problem or a challenge. Then, regardless of what your relationship is to that challenge, just for a moment, treat it as a problem that has to be solved right now. Imagine *pushing against* it. Make something happen. Just fix it. Imagine doing whatever you have to do to make the problem go away so that everything can seem to be OK again.

As you do this, notice what is happening in your body and with your breath. How does it feel to "push against" this issue and try to make something happen? How would you describe your relationship to the problem—how this makes you feel about it? What is your level of inner stress and tension? Stay with this long enough to feel the effects of *pushing against*.

Then when you are ready, shake that feeling out of your body. Take a few deep and full breaths and come back to a neutral feeling inside.

Now let yourself be present with your challenge again. Yet this time, consider that your challenge might have a message for you. Imagine that you could float up high above your situation and see or sense it from a completely new perspective. There is something that actually wants to happen here. What if the problem only exists in order to show you something else? What if the problem is actually trying to help you see another possibility or keep you from taking a wrong step? Keep breathing and let "what wants to happen" show itself to you.

As you sense "what wants to happen," let yourself *flow with* that for the next few minutes. You can always go back to *pushing against* later if you wish, but for now, see what there is for you to discover by *flowing with* what actually wants to happen. Notice what is going on in your body and with your breath. What is different than when you were *pushing against?* What is your level of inner stress and tension now?

Your problem or challenge may still be there. Yet chances are, something is shifting in your relationship to it. This is not a "magic pill" that can just make the problem go away and make everything be right again. However, shifting your relationship to the challenge could completely change how you are approaching it.

"Push Against – Flow With" is a fundamental awareness skill in Transformational Presence. Throughout your day, pause to check in with yourself about how you are being present with whatever is going on. Are you pushing against or are you flowing with? If you are a leader or a coach or work with other people, teach them this simple skill as well. Just the simple reminder to step back from "pushing against," pay attention to the message trying to get through, and breathe into "flowing with" can make a big difference in how your team or organization approaches whatever is happening.

PRINCIPLE #3—The world is built on a matrix of relationships.

"Relationship" can be defined as "a state of connectedness between two or more energies through a physical or a non-physical space." Many people think of relationships as being primarily between people or between living things. Yet we're also talking about relationships between people and ideas, between people and organizations, between ideas and beliefs—the list can go on and on. Everything exists or happens in relationship to something else. Nothing exists or happens in isolation.

The first principle tells us that everything is energy in motion. Therefore, the relationship space is also energy in motion. It's the moving energy within a relationship space that creates the matrix and ties everything together. When the energy shifts in the relationship space, the energy within everything that is connected through that relationship also changes. The relationship space is most often where transformational work happens and where the greatest insights are found.

We begin working with this third principle through a model called the Four Levels of Engagement that I first introduced in my last book, *Create A World That Works*. The purpose of this model is to help you and those you serve make clear choices about how you/they relate to events and situations in daily life.

How we engage with the people and situations in our lives influences the energy of our relationships with them. And we know from the Participant-Observer Principle of quantum physics that how we engage with the energy— how we show up and the presence that we bring to the circumstances and situations of our lives and work—has a significant influence on the quality of the energy itself and the form that emerges.

While we engage with life in many different ways, there are four rather basic levels from which we approach events and circumstances in our lives. I've named these levels:

Drama
Situation
Choice
Opportunity

These Four Levels of Engagement give us a structure for cutting to the essence or core of what is going on as quickly as possible. The simplicity of the model rapidly expands awareness of our relationship to what is happening.

On the surface, right out in front to capture everyone's attention, is the Drama—the level of full-on emotional reaction to what is happening. This is the "oh-my-god-I-can't-believe-this-is-happening-to-me!" level. When we live in Drama, we seem to constantly be "putting out fires." A common first reaction is to look for someone or something else to blame. We take no personal responsibility for what is happening. Our reactive questions might include: Whose fault is this? How did this happen? Can you believe he did that? What were they thinking? Why is this happening to me?

For a very short time, being in the Drama can create an outlet to "blow off steam." Sometimes we just need to tell the story in order to release our pent-up energy and emotions. A quick release can be helpful. However, when we find ourselves telling the story over and over again, the Drama has become a trap. Drama tends to feed on itself and can quickly become a vicious circle, whether within an individual's life, in a family, or in an organization or society. Therefore, the more we can stay out of Drama and drop down to the deeper levels, the better.

The Four Levels of Engagement

Drama

↓

Situation

↓↑

Choice

↓↑

Opportunity

Just below the Drama lies the Situation level. When we drop down into Situation, we have stepped past the "reaction" stage to analyzing what is going on and looking for a solution. At the Situation level, we're looking for the facts—what actually happened. The typical question here is, "How do we fix it?" And the feeling is often, "How do we fix it as quickly as possible so that nobody else knows that this happened?" We may not actually say those words out loud, but that's often an unspoken desire and intention. In Situation, the primary objective is often to make things OK again as quickly as we can, and to control how others perceive what has happened. It's all about returning to "normal." We are eager to move on and put the situation behind us.

Very little, if any, learning happens at the Drama and Situation levels. Most likely, we have just put a bandage on the situation or "swept it under the rug." Therefore, a similar situation or challenge is likely to come up again because the real underlying issues—the messages that were trying to get our attention—were never acknowledged and addressed.

Unfortunately, in our society, the Situation level is often as far as we go. We have been well trained to either look for someone or something else to blame for what happened, or to be good "problem solvers." We approach life from the perspective of, "Things happen to us and we just have to deal with them." We are victims of our circumstances and seem to have no collective awareness that there might be another possibility.

However, if we are willing to go deeper, the third level of Choice invites a shift in consciousness. It's as if we cross a threshold into another level of awareness. By "choice," I'm not speaking about our choices of how to fix what is happening. This third level invites us to make clear choices about who we will be within the situation. It asks us to choose the role we will play and the attitude with which we will approach what is happening. At the Choice level, we recognize that while we cannot control or choose our initial thought when something happens, we *can* choose our second thought. Our first thought often flashes without warning because we're caught by surprise. However, we can learn to catch that first thought and redirect our focus in a way that can serve us. It is the intentional *second* thought that can usher us across the threshold into Choice.

At the Choice level, we learn to ask: Who do I choose to be here? Variations on that question might be: What role have I played in creating this situation, and what role am I playing right now? What role do I *choose* to play going forward? How do I choose to engage with this situation now?

This third level invites us to recognize that, although we may not be able to change our circumstance or situation right away, we can at least choose who we will be within that circumstance. And that's a huge step forward. Now we are claiming responsibility for ourselves, for our choices, and for our actions. We are no longer victims. We are choosing how we will engage and co-create with life rather than allowing life to simply "happen" to us. From this place, we can start to create something new. The door is now open for transformation and sustainable change.

From Choice, we can easily drop down to the fourth level: Opportunity. At the Opportunity level, our first question is: What wants to happen? Now we're getting to the true power within our situation. We acknowledge that this situation happened for a reason, even if we don't yet fully understand what that reason is. We trust that what has happened is trying to tell us something. It's trying to give us a message. And, in fact, there is usually a direct correlation between the Drama and the Opportunity levels: the bigger the drama, the greater the opportunity. The drama is a wake-up call alerting us that something wants to shift or transform.

Once we have identified the Opportunity, we look back to Choice, often with more clarity or insight about who we choose to be within this circumstance and what role we choose to play. And from the awareness that comes from Opportunity and Choice, we look back up to Situation and realize that our relationship to what is happening has shifted.

FOUR LEVELS OF ENGAGEMENT	
Level	Typical Questions
Drama	Whose fault is this? Who can I blame? Can you believe this happened to me/us?
Situation	How can I/we fix it, and how quickly?
Choice	Who do I/we choose to be here? What do I/we choose as my/our relationship to this situation?
Opportunity	What's the opportunity here? What wants to happen? What is the gift that is trying to show itself? What is trying to shift? What breakthrough is trying to happen?

When we engage with life primarily from Drama and Situation, our focus tends to be on struggle and problem solving. It can feel like we're just moving from one challenge or crisis to another. We live in reaction rather than response, giving our power away to something outside of us. As a result, we spin into a downward spiral of our circumstances. However, when we engage with life primarily from Choice and Opportunity, we take our power back. Consciously choosing who we will be in relationship to our circumstances empowers us to break free from struggle and create new realities. We flow with the Opportunity or potential and transform "what is" into "what it wants to be."

Leading and serving from Opportunity cuts to the essence or core of what is going on. Asking, "What wants to happen?" invites everyone involved to a higher level of awareness where learning and forward movement becomes possible. Living from Choice and Opportunity opens the door into much greater insight, awareness, and effective action.

Learning to live and lead from the Choice and Opportunity levels starts with being focused and disciplined enough to step beyond the drama, and then courageous enough to name what is really happening deep at the core of the situation. It starts with being bold enough to *choose who you will be* within your situation and to make your first question: What's the opportunity available now? Or simply: What wants to happen? In this way, you help those you serve engage from Choice and Opportunity as well. It's what "Flow With" is all about.

Introducing the Four Levels of Engagement to your team or organization, and even to your family and friends, can be a simple yet very effective first step towards creating a transformational environment and culture. The Four Levels of Engagement is a simple yet powerful framework to help you quickly cut through to the core or essence of situations and circumstances. It can help you understand your situation more clearly and discover the hidden messages.

Transformational Presence comes out of listening and responding from Choice and Opportunity regardless of where others are. The more you engage life from Choice and Opportunity, the more those you serve will learn to live at these deeper levels of awareness, to approach their situations from Choice and Opportunity, and to radiate a more powerful presence in their lives and work.

Notice as well that our Three Fundamental Principles are all present in this Four Levels of Engagement framework. As we come into Choice and Opportunity, we begin treating what is happening more as energy rather than form (Principle #1). We recognize that "a problem is not something to be solved; it is a message to be listened to" (Principle #2). And as we shift our relationship to what is happening, we see and understand more clearly how to move forward (Principle #3).

In addition, our Three Fundamental Questions are also present as we come from Opportunity back up through Choice to have a new perspective on the Situation.

Clarifying the Opportunity becomes Question #1: What wants to happen?

From that awareness, we come back up into Choice for Question #2: Who is that asking me/us to be?

And then we look back to Situation to ask Question #3: What is that asking me/us to do?

You will find three different ways of introducing the Four Levels of Engagement, whether to an individual or to a team or organization, in the *Tools, Skills, and Frameworks* book.

If the concepts presented in this chapter were familiar to you already, hopefully this has deepened your understanding or awareness in some way. Or perhaps it has given you some practical ways to talk about these concepts with those you serve.

If these concepts and this way of thinking are new for you, take your time here. Keep coming back to his chapter and read from your heart intelligence. Let these concepts sink in. The following chapter, as well as the practical application tools in the *Frameworks* book and at TransformationalPresenceBook.com, will continue to bring these concepts to life.

CHAPTER 5

The Power of Listening and Observing

If you tell life
what it has to be,
you limit it.
If you let it show you
what it wants to be,
it will open doors
you never knew existed.

—Rutter-Rhymer

YEARS AGO ON ONE OF their many trips together, my parents found a whimsical wall hanging made of three ceramic tiles inscribed with the words above. My father pointed out the hanging to my mother and said to her quietly, "That looks like Alan. That's what he's teaching us."

Some months later as my father presented the wall hanging to me as a Christmas gift, he told the story of finding it and recognizing me in it. He went on to say that reading those words helped him more fully understand what my work was all about. His story alone was already a great gift to me. Today, the ceramic tiles hang in the entranceway to my office as a playful reminder of this simple truth, as well as of my father's enduring presence in my life and work.

The simple yet profound concept inscribed on those ceramic tiles expresses the essence of the Three Questions (Chapter 3) and the Three Principles (Chapter 4). However, this concept is not one that most of us have been taught. How many times have you been told that you should have a clear picture of what you want, set goals to get there, design a plan to make it happen, and then actively implement your plan?

There is nothing wrong with setting goals, making plans, and then moving into action! Having a sense of direction and actively moving forward in that direction are essential if you want to make a meaningful difference in the world.

However, *telling life what it has to be* and then doing whatever it takes to make that happen can significantly limit our possibilities. It can also lead to a lot of unnecessary pressure and stress.

Not only is there an easier way—there is also a more productive and fulfilling way that can bring results far beyond anything we could have imagined. It's not magic or a secret formula. It's just a different approach than what many of us have been taught. It starts with the awareness that your circumstance, situation, or project probably has something to say to you—that it has information that can be helpful to you, and that can guide you forward.

In concluding our discussion of the Second Principle in the last chapter, we worked with the simple coaching process, "Push Against – Flow With." Just to review, instead of "pushing against" our circumstance or trying to manipulate it into something else, the idea is to step back and pay attention to what is happening underneath the surface. Chances are there is a message that will give you clues about your next steps.

Also remember that "flow with" is not the same thing as "go with the flow." "Go with the flow" is choosing to give in to whatever is currently happening. When we do this, we stop taking responsibility for what is happening and just let the situation unfold as it will. In some circumstances, that might be OK, yet in others, as you have probably experienced, it doesn't turn out so well.

"Flow with" is a proactive approach that starts with tapping into the greater potential waiting to unfold—"what wants to happen" in service of something bigger than you or your organization—and following that potential towards a greater outcome.

In this chapter, we anchor the learning from the last few chapters and bring it all together in what is perhaps the central message of this book: If we pause to pay attention to the signals, there are messages everywhere. And if we pay attention to those messages and remain curious and open-minded, they will show us the way forward, even when things are breaking open, even in a VUCA world.

Just as the message on the ceramic tiles says, most of us have been conditioned to *talk to life* (push against) much more than to *let life talk to us* (flow with). In other words, we tell life what we want it to be, we tell our situations what we think needs to happen, and we control our experiences as much as possible so that we remain safely within our comfort zones.

So let's bring the Three Questions and the Three Principles together in practical application. Consider a challenge or an opportunity that is showing up in your life or work right now. Pause from your reading just long enough to choose your "topic." Then once you have chosen your topic, continue reading as if you and I were having a mini-coaching session. When I ask a question, pause your reading just long enough to answer the question, and then continue on. You can also find a video that will lead you through this mini-coaching process at Transformational-PresenceBook.com.

Let's begin this mini-coaching session by looking at how you are approaching your topic. At the most fundamental level, are you talking to it—telling it what you need or want and trying to make something happen—or are you stepping back to listen and invite your topic to talk to you?

Whatever your answer is, it's OK. We're just gathering information. Our first objective in this exploration is to notice the general direction of your communication. Is the communication flowing mostly from you to your topic, or from your topic to you?

When we're in "push against" mode, we're talking to it, and often we're trying to make something happen. Our "manipulation" may be very subtle, yet if we are honest with ourselves, it's there. When we're in "flow with" mode, we're much more receptive and can let the topic talk to us.

Notice what happens in your relationship to your topic when you let it talk to you. Don't worry about how to do that—just assume that you know how and see what happens. Let the communication come in whatever way feels the most natural for you. You might sense or feel something, you might get visual images, or you might hear words or phrases. Or perhaps even some combination of all three. Again, take your time.

As you gather information from your topic, resist the temptation to respond by telling it what you want or what you think. Continue to be curious. Ask another question and give your topic time to respond. Ask your topic what it wants you to know. Ask it to show you what's important to pay attention to right now. Let your topic show you something that you haven't yet realized—something that wants to happen or a potential that is waiting to emerge. Pause from your reading. What are you discovering? What is shifting in your relationship to your topic and your understanding of it? Take your time, and continue with our mini-coaching session when you are ready.

Now leave that topic and consider a goal or a project that you want to accomplish. Pay attention again—have you been talking to it, or asking it to talk to you? Be honest with yourself and make no judgments. You're just gathering information. If you recognize that the energy has been flowing primarily from you to the project, turn that around. What does the project want to say to you? Who is it asking you to be? What is it asking you to do? Just notice what information is available. And notice what is shifting in your relationship to the project as you open this communication flow. Again, take your time.

When you are ready, leave that goal or project and choose a relationship that is important to you. Bring in the relationship itself, not just the other person or people. The relationship has its own space and energy. Notice your habitual way of being with this relationship. Do you tell the relationship what you want it to be? Do you impose your energy and wishes on the relationship, or do you let the relationship talk to you?

You might want to take a few minutes to reflect on your insights from this exploration before you continue reading.

≋

When I lead this exploration in a workshop, most participants discover right away that their habitual approach is to *talk to* their topic. We have been conditioned to operate primarily in "output" mode—to *talk to* people, circumstances, situations, challenges, or possibilities. We are rewarded for making things happen, fixing what is not working, and getting results. For most of us, stepping back, listening, and observing—stepping into "receptive" mode—has not been a part of our training. The invitation of Transformational Presence is to be in a receptive and interactive space—to enter fully into dialogue with our circumstances and situations and to let them talk to us.

Even when a few participants acknowledge the value of letting their challenge or situation talk to them, they still admit that, too often, the pressure or inner desire to get to an outcome quickly overrides their inner knowing. Our conditioning to make something happen or create a specific result is really strong!

Carolyn, a high-level executive, shared her insights and discoveries. "Through this exercise, I'm realizing that when I accept responsibility for something, I usually feel like I must control what happens. Other people are counting on me. So I *talk to* the situation and even sometimes try to force an outcome that I think is best. However, through this exercise, I'm discovering a whole new way of being *responsive*. I'm starting to understand that I can probably be more effective and impactful when my initial *response* to what is happening is to let the situation *talk to me*. I'm seeing how I need to put 'responsive' back into 'responsibility.' My efforts to control the outcome have been rooted in good and honorable intentions. However, now I realize that when I don't *listen* first, I'm missing out on important and often valuable information or messages that are trying to get through."

Many people associate the word "responsibility" with carrying a heavy weight. Yet when we define "responsibility" as our "ability to respond," the meaning is transformed. From this perspective, when we take on a particular responsibility, we're actually exercising our ability to respond to what wants to happen and then to make choices and actions accordingly.

Viktor, a division manager, shared, "Now I recognize that, on the surface, *talking to* the situation and taking control of things makes me feel good because I feel large and in charge and powerful. However, this exercise is showing me that being in receptive mode is actually much more powerful. It's going to take practice. I'll have to take time to silence my old habits and become curious. Yet I think it's going to feel even more amazing because I'm going to be more effective."

As you invite your topic, situation, or circumstance to talk to you, the messages or answers may not always come right away or in the forms that you expect. Often messages come as metaphors or symbols, and they may show up in unrelated conversations or events hours or even days later. Someone may make a passing comment that appears to come out of nowhere, yet it has a clear meaning for you. Or you may walk past a newsstand and a headline catches your attention. Or the lyrics of a song that you haven't thought about for a long time suddenly keep playing over and over again in your head.

Jackie, a coach, said, "Listening opens up my 'not knowing' much more and asks me to trust what is being revealed through the listening. It's powerful and exciting and scary at the same time. And then I have to be careful that, once I go into action, I don't revert to my 'push against' and 'talk to' habit."

Robert, a project manager, lit up with amazement as he discovered, "It can change from moment to moment. One moment I'm 'talking to,' and the next moment I'm 'listening to.' It's a full circle. This is incredible. My project and I are talking to each other. The project is answering my questions and showing me where to go next. I would never have imagined that this was possible!" Marsha, a new CEO, added to Robert's discovery: "I have to combine doing with listening. Now I see that they can be partners. I'm learning that we can receive and act at the same time. This is the new way to lead."

Ultimately, as both Robert and Marsha discovered, it is a dialogue. We listen, sense, and feel first—we let life talk to us. And then, we respond, perhaps through an action, or by asking a question, or making a request. And then we listen again. We are at our best in life, leadership, and service when we let ourselves be guided by our open dialogue with what is happening.

Making a difference begins with paying attention. There are messages everywhere. Our job is to be open and receptive. Being open and receptive may also require letting go of our personal agendas. We all have our own wants and needs in life. We're human. Yet attachment to particular outcomes can keep us from noticing the important messages that are trying to come through.

Towards the end of another workshop session, Frank, a successful entrepreneur, said, "I realize that I have to let go of my 'conditions' in order to be the most receptive. I have to practice constantly becoming the next more open version of myself. When I see everything as energy, life is so much more fluid. It's so clear to me now that fluidity is the key! Life is fluid. It's just energy in motion. It's not fixed. Yet I've looked at circumstances as 'fixed things' instead of as 'fluid flows.'

It's completely different when I look at what is happening as a 'fluid flow.' Now I understand more about the 'presence' in Transformational Presence."

Letting go of your agenda requires having faith that the things that need to happen will, in fact, happen, even if not in the way that you had expected. That's not always easy. Two questions that can be helpful in letting go of our prior agendas are:

- Who might you be without the "need" or "want" that you feel right now?

- What might be possible if you were to let go of your agenda?

Trust doesn't happen overnight. It takes time and it takes practice. Start practicing with circumstances and situations where the stakes are not so high. Give yourself time to get used to new ideas, thoughts, feelings, and approaches. And at the same time, keep your focus and keep moving forward.

Harry, an executive coach, summed it up in these words: "What I have learned through this exercise—to let the situation, project, challenge, or opportunity *talk to me*—is actually the most powerful key to carrying the world forward in a healthy, sustainable way."

It's really pretty simple. There are just Three Fundamental Principles:

1) Everything is energy in motion, a part of a larger process unfolding. Form follows energy.

2) Energy cannot be created or destroyed; it can only be transformed.

3) The world is built on a matrix of relationships.

And there are just Three Questions:

1) What wants to happen?

2) Who is that asking me/us to be?

3) What is it asking me/us to do?

The Three Principles and Three Questions all come together in our very simple Transformational Presence Model:

Opportunity → Presence → Action

Transformational Presence means living in a constant dialogue with everything that is around us and within us. There is information everywhere. With practice, we can learn to listen, sense, feel, and intuit what situations and circumstances are trying to show us or tell us and to respond with openness and curiosity.

In the next chapter, we'll go deeper into how to listen, sense, feel, and intuit.

CHAPTER 6

Whole-Mind Thinking and Whole-Being Awareness

It is always with excitement that I wake up in the morning
wondering what my intuition will toss up to me, like gifts from the sea.
I work with it and rely on it. It's my partner.
Intuition will tell the thinking mind where to look next.

—Jonas Salk
American medical researcher and virologist,
developer of the first successful polio vaccine

THERE IS A UNIVERSAL SAYING, "The answers are within." Often, this saying is interpreted to mean that the answers are within *us*—that we have everything we need inside of us. However, this interpretation is actually not fully accurate. The answers themselves are not always within us. Yet what *is* within us is a technology that can help us find the answers that we need. That technology lies within our human energy system.

The universal saying, "The answers are within," comes from the Principle of Polarity, which we have already spoken about. As a reminder, the Principle of Polarity says that a circumstance or feeling cannot exist unless the possibility for its opposite is also present. In practical application, that means that a question cannot exist unless the answer is also present. A challenge cannot exist unless the resolution is also possible. A problem cannot exist unless the optimal solution is available.

However, unless the situation has to do with our own emotions or feelings, that "something else" that wants to happen or the answer that we seek may not lie *inside of us*. Chances are, it actually lies somewhere within the field of information that is currently manifesting as the particular circumstance or situation that we find ourselves in.

We have said that everything is made up of vibrating energy. That includes us. Our human energy system is actually a field of information that is constantly engaging and interacting with the field of information around whatever is happening. Our human energy technology is our primary tool for sensing, intuiting, or perceiving information. It's our technology for discovery and awareness. Through our human energy technology, we have within us an innate ability to sense or uncover the answers that lie within the field of information that makes up our circumstance. A significant part of what makes someone's presence transformational is his or her ability to access and work with their innate human energy technology to access that field of information.

In Transformational Presence work, we call this technology **Whole-Mind Thinking** and **Whole-Being Awareness**. It's an "awareness" technology that allows us to access the information that is all around us and within us. It allows us to sense the messages and potential that lie within our circumstances and situations, and partner with that potential to create something new. Our human energy systems know how to do this already. However, many of us have lost our connection to that knowledge and skill. Through our simple and practical tools and frameworks, the Transformational Presence approach re-awakens that connection.

Whole-Mind Thinking occurs when the intuitive and intellectual minds become partners. This partnership actually exists within us already. However, through our socialization and traditional education experiences, most of us have been conditioned to believe that these two minds are separate. Furthermore, we've been conditioned to believe that the intellect is the one that counts.

The first step in developing Whole-Mind Thinking is the understanding that the intuitive mind is the larger and more powerful mind. The intellectual mind is actually just one aspect of the much larger intuitive mind. *Both are essential* for leadership and service in today's rapidly changing and unpredictable world. They each play critical roles. Understanding those roles is an important step in developing new life and leadership skills and capacities.

In Chapter 2, we spoke about the research on the intelligence of the heart and the intuitive mind at the Institute of HeartMath in Boulder Creek, California (heartmath. org). Since 1991, their scientists have been doing extensive research on the intelligence of the heart and the intuitive mind. You may remember that through their research, they discovered that the electromagnetic field of the heart is five thousand times greater than the electromagnetic field of the brain. The heart is the center of the intuitive mind, while the brain is the center of the intellectual mind. This research helps us understand that the intuitive mind has access to a field of information that is five thousand times greater than the field of information accessible by the intellect alone.

Let's pick up from that discussion in Chapter 2 and go a little deeper. The highly developed intuitive mind is constantly gathering information. It picks up signals from our inner emotions and feelings as well as from what is happening around us. It even senses what is waiting to unfold. In all kinds of circumstances and situations, the intuitive mind senses things that the rational-intellectual mind might miss—things that are happening beneath the surface or that are not so obvious to everyone. It senses "what wants to happen" in the big-picture view. It sees and understands things within a much larger context. It's our inner radar system, feeding us information on everything that is happening, both seen and unseen, and how it is all connected, all the time.

However, while the intuitive mind is very good at gathering information, it's not very good at *organizing* it. For that, it needs the assistance of a really sharp intellect. The well-developed intellect has an incredible mental filing system that allows us to access information from our knowledge, memory, and experience banks very quickly. In simple terms, you could say that the intuitive mind is the explorer and information gatherer, and the intellectual mind is the organizer and cataloger. The intuitive mind sees, feels, and understands the big picture and has an inner knowing or sensing about what we need to do and where we need to go next. The intellect can then step in to take care of the details.

Whole-Being Awareness stretches Whole-Mind Thinking to include the incredible innate awareness, understanding, and wisdom available to us through our human energy system. Perhaps you've heard the saying, "The body knows," or, "The body doesn't lie." When we say, "The body knows," what we are actually saying is that the body is an energy system and technology that can interact with the field of information of a circumstance or situation to understand more clearly what is really happening. This energy system receives insights, clues, and direction for what to do or where to go next.

In the last chapter, we explored how it feels and what becomes possible when we approach things from "receptive" mode before stepping into "output" mode. Being in receptive mode connects you to your human energy technology. When you use your receptors first and let the information that comes in guide your output, great things can happen. However, when you are in output mode alone without the aid and guidance of your receptive capacities, you limit your perceptual awareness to what you can access through your intellect alone. The key, ultimately, as Jackie said in the last chapter, is to remain in receptive mode even when you are in action. Then you are able to experience a constant flow of communication, awareness, and understanding between multiple fields of information.

As Whole-Mind Thinking and Whole-Being Awareness become your default approach to life and leadership, you discover that you have a greater ability to see the "big picture" of what is happening and understand events and circumstances within a much larger context. You learn to recognize patterns and flows of energy and discover how to navigate complex situations.

When faced with challenges, difficulties, or confusion, Whole-Mind Thinking and Whole-Being Awareness reduce stress and foster resilience by transforming your relationship to what is happening. As we said in our mini-coaching sessions in Chapters 4 and 5, there are no magic pills. Yet as your perception and understanding of what is happening expands, you are able to see things within a larger context. Clarity emerges, and you sense what to do next.

Coming back to the beginning of this chapter, the more accurate interpretation of "the answers are within" is that *the answers are within what is happening.* They are within the energy field of the situation or circumstance. If the situation or circumstance is something inside of you, then the answers will be found there as well. However, if your challenge is within a project or a relationship or a societal issue, the *answers* may not be within you. They will be within the situation itself. Within *you* is an extraordinary awareness technology that can help you discover or uncover the answers or next steps that are waiting to be found in the energy field of the situation.

The Transformational Presence approach calls us home to our innate human energy technology. Whole-Mind Thinking and Whole-Being Awareness are our most natural ways of being and sensing. They are our human energy system coming alive. When we expand far beyond the intellect into the vastness of the intuitive mind, we are able to access the quantum field. We can access the greater Consciousness. As you share this approach with your colleagues and the people you serve, the collective thinking, inquiry, perception, and understanding of the team or organization expands. The companion *Frameworks* book is filled with tools and exercises to help you and those you serve further develop your Whole-Mind Thinking and Whole-Being Awareness skills and capacities. You will also find many resources at TransformationalPresenceBook.com.

As a culture, we're just beginning to tap the surface of this extraordinary technology. It is capable of guiding and supporting us far more than most people have imagined. While this way of living is not yet fully supported by the mass consciousness, it is a significant key to the *evolution* of the mass consciousness.

In the next chapter, we delve into the distinction between "complicated" and "complex" situations and circumstances, making clear why Whole-Mind Thinking and Whole-Being Awareness are critical skills for navigating today's VUCA world.

CHAPTER 7

Complicated, Complex, Or Both—
Critical Distinctions In a New World

We are moving from a context of "Leading when I know" or when I
should have known, where strategy means guessing the future, to a world
of "Leading when I don't know," where strategizing means preparing
ourselves for whatever future comes our way.

—Didier Marlier
Managing Partner at Enablers Network in Switzerland
from his November 28, 2014 blog post

THROUGHOUT THE BOOK, WE'VE BEEN talking about navigating a VUCA world and the Great Breaking Open. Let's take another step in understanding what makes today's world different and why the Transformational Presence approach is now critical.

In the mid-1960s, Bob Dylan's song, "The Times They Are A-Changin,'" became an anti-establishment anthem for frustrated young people. It carried a prophetic message that could have been both an ominous warning and a hopeful invitation. Looking back now from today's context, his song feels somehow gentle and naïve. It was a simpler time.

Fifty years later, the times are no longer "a-changin;" the times *have* changed—radically. Our world is anything but simple. In fact, rapid, continuous, unpredictable change is the "new normal." Complexity has become the order of the day at every level of society, from family systems to global systems. It's a VUCA world—a world that feels increasingly edgy, unpredictable, chaotic, and, for some, unsafe.

Too often, we find ourselves not knowing how to move forward, whether at the societal level or the personal level. It has become painfully clear that the systems, approaches, guidelines, formulas, and conventional wisdom that we have relied on for so long are no longer working. In fact, the more we try to "fix" things or to "get things under control" again, the more "out of control" things become.

In frustration, many people ask: Why isn't this working? What is the world coming to? How can we just make everything OK again?

Yet as the conscious leadership movement spreads, more people are starting to ask: How do we *respond* to all that is happening? What needs to shift in how we think about and approach leadership and service?

While there are no simple or definitive answers, our Three Questions from Chapter 3 can be a powerful way to begin. And there is also another simple, yet not-so-obvious question that can at least steer us towards an effective approach:

Is this situation complicated or is it complex?

The words complicated and complex are often used interchangeably in everyday conversation. However, they actually describe two different kinds of realities that require two very different kinds of approaches—two very different skill sets. Understanding the difference and recognizing whether a situation is complicated or complex is critical as we navigate today's uncertain and rapidly changing world. When a circumstance or situation is **complicated**, it is possible to "think" our way through it—to analyze it and figure it out. Complicated issues are like a tangled knot or ball of string. It might take some knowledge and expertise to figure them out, as well as a lot of patience if there are multiple layers of "knotted string." Yet with some time and energy, we can resolve them. With the proper knowledge and experience, it is possible to identify all of the pieces or components, figure out how they relate to each other, and how to work with them.

Think of the wiring in your house. While you may not be able to figure out the issue on your own, an experienced electrician can usually track down the problem and solve it. Or perhaps there is a problem in a software program you are using. There might be layers of complication in this kind of issue, yet a software expert can usually find the root of the problem and resolve it.

In **complicated** situations, there is usually an identifiable linear, cause-and-effect sequence of events, choices, or actions that led to what is happening now. The environment around the issue is usually fairly stable and somewhat predictable, and there is often general agreement among the people involved about what the desired outcome is. Complicated situations can usually be resolved through a solution-focused approach.

In **complicated** situations, it is not unreasonable to expect leaders to have answers to our questions. We hope that they are able to clearly define the problems at hand and know how to solve them, or at least know whom to ask for help.

Hopefully, those leaders have risen to their positions because of their experience, knowledge, and expertise in their fields. Therefore, within this context, we might expect our leaders to develop clear visions for the future and to design clear strategies for making things happen.

However, when a situation or circumstance is **complex**, much of the above no longer applies. There are likely to be many moving pieces, and those pieces may be constantly changing, evolving, or morphing into other forms. Conditions are constantly shifting, and there may be many different ideas and opinions about what the outcomes should be. Often, many things are happening at once. We might sense that some of these things are related to one another, yet the connections between them are not obvious. Very little is predictable, and there is no clear cause-and-effect sequence. The ground beneath our feet keeps shifting and movement patterns tend to be circular or erratic instead of linear. The whole environment can feel unstable.

In **complex** situations, our past knowledge and experience is often no longer relevant. The ways that things worked before is not necessarily how they will work again. Therefore, making a plan is challenging, if not impossible. Everything keeps moving and changing. Usually, the best you can do when working in complexity is to look for your next step, take that step, and then observe what happens as a result. What you learn or discover through that observation then informs your next step. After you take that step, you pause to sense what is next. And you continue repeating this cycle as long as necessary.

Complex situations need leaders with great capacity for Whole-Mind Thinking and Whole-Being Awareness. They need leaders who are skilled at navigating uncertainty, volatility, and rapid change—leaders who understand how the world works as energy in motion. Therefore, when working in complexity, our expectations from leaders must be different than when we are working in complicated situations. Expecting leaders to have all the answers, to clearly define what is happening, and to know what to do is not realistic. That's not how complexity works.

Characteristics of Complicated and Complex Systems and Situations

COMPLICATED	COMPLEX
There is a predictable, cause-and-effect sequence.	Very little is predictable—there is no obvious cause-and-effect sequence.
Movement patterns are linear.	Movement patterns are circular and erratic—rarely linear.
You can identify all of the pieces or components and figure out how to work with them and how they relate to each other.	There are many moving pieces that are constantly changing. Many things are happening at once, yet the connections between them are often not obvious.
You can "think" your way through it—you can analyze it and figure it out.	You must be able to "read the signals." The situation demands Whole-Mind Thinking and Whole-Being Awareness.

COMPLICATED	COMPLEX
You can make a plan and more or less follow the plan to success.	Making a plan is challenging, if not impossible, because all of the pieces keep moving and changing. Therefore, you can only look for your next step, act, and then stand aside to observe the new or different patterns that emerge, and then take another step. The cycle then continues to repeat until it is no longer needed.
Past knowledge and experience is valuable and serves you well.	Past knowledge and experience are often no longer relevant—how it worked before will not necessarily work again.
The environment tends to be stable.	The environment tends to be less predictable and sometimes unstable.
There is general agreement about the desired outcome.	There are often many different opinions or desires about what the outcome should be.
You are working toward a specific outcome or creating a specific result. It's a solution-focused approach.	The outcome or result will be revealed over time. It's helpful to have a sense of direction, yet that will not always be clear, especially at first. However, commitment or attachment to a specific outcome or result rarely serves in a complex situation.

COMPLICATED	COMPLEX
The "complicated" label tends to apply primarily to mechanical or technical issues or systems, or to tasks that will be served by logical, linear approaches, and where you can reasonably expect predictable outcomes.	The "complex" label tends to apply to situations that involve people's feelings, values, and emotions; personal or professional relationships; or organizational or societal systems.

In navigating **complicated** situations, it's helpful to be analytical and systematic. However, in **complex** situations, we need to be intuitive, creative, imaginative, innovative, and flexible. We need to be able to respond quickly to what is happening in the moment. Instead of having all of the answers, we learn to be comfortable in the "not knowing." It's important to give ourselves, as well as others, permission to try something new, fully knowing that it may or may not work. Exploration and experimentation should be encouraged and supported. Rather than viewing outcomes from a perspective of success or failure, it's more helpful to look at them from the perspective of, "What are we learning; what do we choose to carry forward; and what do we choose to leave behind?"

Navigating complexity requires being able to see beneath the surface—to perceive beyond the obvious—and dance with both the big picture and the details at the same time. It involves sensing when to pause, giving things time to come together or fall into place, and when to move ahead in decisive action. The system or the circumstance itself becomes our guide and teacher, even as it changes and evolves.

From a quantum physics perspective, the **complicated** world operates primarily in the "particle" state of fixed forms. The **complex** world, on the other hand, operates much more in the "wave" state—a state of constantly moving energy where anything is possible. The more we understand life, relationships, societal systems, and organizational structures as energy in motion, the clearer we become about how to navigate a complex world.

In the last chapter, we talked about the intellectual and intuitive minds and how they have different, yet very complementary, strengths. We talked about the importance of their partnership, and at the same time, the importance of the intuitive mind leading the way.

This is particularly true when working in **complexity**. Complex situations are often confusing and overwhelming to the intellect. The intellect longs for order—for all of the pieces to fit together into a linear, organized, consistent structure. It wants to be able to control and predict what is going to happen. However, in a complex system, linear sequence and predictable patterns are the exception, not the rule. The intellectual mind alone cannot grasp the many moving pieces and shifting patterns of complexity.

The larger intuitive mind, on the other hand, has a much greater capacity for handling complexity. It is designed to explore and discover, to observe what is happening, to look for and recognize emerging patterns, to sense the hidden messages, and to "connect the dots" between what might appear on the surface to be unrelated circumstances and events. The intuitive mind can then sense how to respond and discern what the next step might be.

In an unexpected sort of way, there is actually simplicity within complexity. Approaching complexity with complexity will not get us very far. However, approaching complexity with simple, direct, and powerful questions can often cut through to the essence and begin to open up some space within the complexity so that we can begin to see our way through it. This is because simple yet powerful questions can take us directly to the greater awareness of the intuitive mind.

This intuitive approach to complex situations can feel counter-intellectual. It's a completely different approach than many of us are used to. Yet if we give it a chance, some bigger part of us—our intuitive selves—comes alive. To the intuitive mind and heart intelligence, this approach feels quite natural. We expand way beyond our intellectual expertise into Whole-Mind Thinking and Whole-Being Awareness. We become experts at perceiving energy and information, receiving guidance, sensing next steps, and moving into action.

To the intuitive mind, complexity is not a mystery, nor is it overwhelming. It's just a different reality that requires a different set of skills and capacities—the skills and capacities that come from Whole-Mind Thinking and Whole-Being Awareness. The key is to stay in "receptive" mode rather than fall back into "output" or "figure it out" mode. Start by asking: What is trying to get my/our attention right now? What is this situation trying to tell or show me/us? What potential is trying to emerge? What wants to happen? In other words, we come back to the Three Questions.

An expansion on the Three Questions can be found in a framework I call "The Deep Simple." I designed this tool or framework for those times when the situation or circumstance is so complex that you have no idea where to begin.

"The Deep Simple" is a series of five powerful questions that can help you cut through the confusion and find a next step. The questions are:

1) What are three things that you know to be true with this circumstance or situation?

2) Which of those things holds the most power to explore right now?

3) With that thing that holds the most power, what wants to shift? What is the breakthrough waiting to happen or the potential waiting to emerge?

4) Who is that shift asking you to be? What role is it asking you to play?

5) What is one step that you can take today to begin moving toward that shift?

In the first question, we're asking only about what is true for you or for your team right now. It's not "True" with a capital "T"—it's simply your perception. What is true for you right now?

Notice in the second question that we are not asking, "Which of those three things do you *want* to explore or work with?" We're asking, "Which one holds the power?" In other words, which one seems to have the greatest control over the situation right now? Or which one would be most helpful to address first?

Questions 3, 4, and 5 are then variations on our Three Questions. Notice in the last question that we are not asking how we can resolve the issue. We're just asking for one step that can move us toward the shift that wants to happen. All we're looking for is one small step that we can take today. The "Deep Simple" helps us break down the complexity into manageable pieces. It relieves stress and overwhelm. And it shows us our next step.

Once you have taken that step, go back to Question #1 again. Now that you have taken that step, what are three things that you know to be true? And continue through the sequence again. Continue working in this simple approach and you will find your way forward.

You will find more about "The Deep Simple" in the companion *Frameworks* book as well as at TransformationalPresenceBook.com.

Comparison Approaches
for Complicated and Complex Situations

COMPLICATED APPROACH	COMPLEX APPROACH
An intellectual, rational, analytical, linear, clear, practical approach is best.	An intuitive, creative, imaginative, innovative, flexible, exploratory approach is needed—Whole-Mind Thinking and Whole-Being Awareness.
Past knowledge and skills are important and valuable.	Become comfortable in "not knowing"—living in space of discovery.
Use your analyzing skills to fix the situation. Look for a linear cause-and-effect sequence and create the sequence going forward that is likely to resolve the issue.	Dance with the big picture *and* with the details at the same time, and dance in the constant movement between them. Start with the Deep Simple and begin to find your way, one step at a time. You are looking for patterns and flows of energy rather than linear cause and effect. Cause and effect will rarely be obvious, even in retrospect. You have to look beneath the surface.
Make a plan and implement it, and don't stop until it's done.	There is a rhythm and flow to how things will want to unfold. It's important to be able to sense when to move ahead and when to pause or step back, or even take a different approach.

COMPLICATED APPROACH	COMPLEX APPROACH
Because we are working in the realm of "particle" or fixed forms, follow the rules of the 3-dimensional world and classical physics.	You are working in the wave where things are constantly moving and shifting. Anything is possible. Understanding everything as energy in motion is critical. The rules of quantum physics and a 4-dimensional world and beyond now apply.
It's all about planning and implementation.	It's all about discovery and navigation.

As we wrap up this chapter, consider some of the current situations and circumstances in your life and work. Notice which situations feel **complicated**—primarily linear and predictable. What do you know already about how to resolve these situations? Make a few notes about your next steps. Perhaps even start the outline of a plan or strategy to move forward.

Then notice which situations feel primarily **complex** and unpredictable, confusing and maybe even overwhelming. Choose one to focus on for the next few minutes. Then imagine that this complex situation is in the room with you. Take a moment to feel the energy of this situation. You don't have to do anything with it—just let yourself be present with it. Then, instead of trying to figure it out or make a plan to fix it, step into receptive mode. Listen, observe, and sense what wants to happen next. Use the "Deep Simple" to help you find your next step. Remember that you're not trying to solve the whole puzzle or get a quick result.

Complex situations don't work that way. You're just looking for your next step.

When you finish reading this chapter, you might even take a break and go for a walk. Invite your complex situation to walk with you. Listen to it. Sense it. Let it talk to you. Use the structure of the "Deep Simple" to support your discovery process. Give yourself permission to not know the answers and, instead, let the answers show themselves to you. Trust that something wants to happen and that it can lead you forward.

〰

In reality, many circumstances and situations have both complicated *and* complex elements. There is even a new word emerging in the lexicon to describe these kinds of situations: *complexicated*. Navigating today's VUCA world actually requires being able to distinguish which elements are complicated and which are complex, recognize the appropriate approach, and then be able to shift from one approach to the other quickly and easily as you move between the different elements of your situation.

Becoming a master at navigating complexity means staying in discovery rather than trying to "figure out" what to do next. The more agile you become in Whole-Mind Thinking and Whole-Being Awareness, the more smoothly you will find your way through complex situations and circumstances. It just takes awareness and practice.

To summarize, complicated and complex situations ask for two different kinds of approaches. When the situation is **complicated**, it is helpful to be rational, analytical, linear, clear, and practical as you address what is going on. Tap into your past knowledge and skills. Look for linear cause-and-effect sequences or patterns to understand how the situation evolved to where it is now. And then make a step-by-step plan for moving into action. When the situation is **complex**, a rational, analytical, and linear approach will not serve you. In fact, it will often make things even worse. Tap into your Whole-Mind Thinking and Whole-Being Awareness skills—your intuitive, creative, imaginative, innovative, flexible, and explorer side. Get comfortable with not knowing the answers, and maybe not even knowing the questions. Be curious and open to discovery. Start with the Three Questions or the "Deep Simple," and you will begin to find your way. Remember that you are looking for patterns and flows of energy rather than linear patterns of cause and effect. Look, sense, and feel beneath the surface.

The world is likely to keep moving and changing quickly, so learning to dance with the big picture and the details at the same time is critical. There is a constant movement between them. Allow yourself to *flow with* that movement rather than push against it or try to hold it still. A rhythm and flow to how things want to unfold will start to be revealed. As you dance with that flow, you will sense when to move ahead and when to pause, step back, or even shift to a different approach. "What wants to happen" will guide you if you pay attention.

In the next chapter, we explore why we resist complexity, both individually and collectively, and how we can move past that resistance.

CHAPTER 8

Why We Resist Complexity and Why Embracing It Is Critical

Everything should be made as simple as possible, but not simpler.

—Albert Einstein

HOW WE AS A SOCIETY respond to the Great Breaking Open and the deep complexity of our times will determine how we move forward as a collective. From the outset, let me say that it is not my intention in this chapter to criticize, but rather to objectively acknowledge what has been happening on a broad scale. My intention is to treat what is happening as information rather than judging it as right or wrong, and to explore where we might go from here.

Generally speaking, when we, both as individuals and as a society, sense that something important to us is breaking down or falling apart, a common reaction is to ignore or deny the deeper complex issues behind what is happening. Too often, we either attempt to rationalize the situation away, or we look for the quickest fix. Rarely do we actually address what is going on under the surface. Rather than judging ourselves or others for this response, let's look at what causes our resistance to addressing the deeper layers of our situations and circumstances and how we might move past that resistance.

As a human species, when we feel threatened, our survival instincts of fear and urgency kick in. In those moments, we are often bombarded with information, feelings, and emotions, and we become easily overwhelmed. Our survival self takes over, and our mental and emotional bandwidth is reduced to seeing everything in binary terms. We can only perceive what is happening in yes-or-no, black-or-white, right-or-wrong, us-versus-them terms. The survival self has little capacity for a big-picture view. It has little concern for the thoughts and feelings of others beyond those that it is protecting. Nor does it have capacity for considering the long-term consequences of choices and actions. We make quick assumptions about who is with us and who is with the enemy. We want to know right away who we can count on to support us and whom we can't.

At the same time, the survivor self wants to appear to be in control. It will go to great lengths to assure others that everything is fine. And it may even make valiant efforts to convince itself that no one else can see or feel its inner fears. Meanwhile, those inner fears cut deeper and deeper into our psyche.

When this happens on a societal level, the collective survival self begins oversimplifying and even "dumbing down" the issues in order to convince the masses to support its position. And this is where things start to get dangerous. The more we disregard the full spectrum of what is going on and the feelings and emotions that are present within what is happening, the more we bury layer upon layer of conflicting emotions, opinions, feelings, hopes, and dreams.

In a relatively short time, this creates an incredibly confusing matrix of complexity.

For example, the deep polarization between liberal and conservative, progressive and traditional, globalist and nationalist, has resulted from both sides making broad assumptions about people on the other side. As a mass culture, we have become so accustomed to the oversimplified positions of sound bites and vilifying those from the other side for their beliefs, perspectives, and intentions, that we stop noticing what is actually happening. As a result, neither side can hear the other. Deeper thoughts, feelings, circumstances, hopes, and dreams are ignored, including our own. The collective survival self is so busy *pushing against* the perceived enemy that it loses touch with what its true values and heart feelings are.

This is the matrix of complexity that we as a society are living in now. It has become our reality. And this reality has become increasingly cloudy and opaque, unpredictable and volatile, confusing and overwhelming. It's a VUCA world.

Because it takes significant effort, attention, and focus from an open mind and heart to fully comprehend all that is going on, it's no wonder that the general reaction from a large segment of the population is to reduce overwhelming complexity to simple either-or scenarios. The survivor self has great difficulty coping with what is happening. Its job is to make sure we are safe—that nothing bad will happen to us. Reducing life to "yes-or-no" or "this-or-that" choices is the survival self's way of attempting to manage the confusing and overwhelming situation.

However, an either-or approach only works in **complicated** situations—situations that are somewhat linear and predictable in nature. There is very little that is linear and predictable about where we are now. We have crossed the line from living in a **complicated** world to living in a **complex** world. Instead of being linear and predictable, complex situations are a matrix of swirling energies, events, emotions, and constantly changing circumstances. Instead of black and white, we have entered the land of a million shades of gray. Very little, if anything, is certain. The ground beneath our feet is constantly shifting. "Yes *or* no" has become "yes *and* no." "Either-or" has become "some of both."

Even defining "reality" becomes difficult. We think of reality as what is actually happening. Yet in truth, it's our *interpretation* of what is happening that creates our "reality" of the situation. Our interpretation can be shaped by:

- Where we are standing at the moment

- The angle from which we are looking at things

- The role or roles we are playing within the situation

- What we perceive to be our pressing needs and/or the needs of others we care about

- Our past experiences

- Our dreams for the future

- Who we allow to influence our thinking

- And the list goes on...

We can easily get so lost in our own realities, both individually and collectively, that we lose touch with the fact that there are other groups of people who are in different circumstances, experiencing different realities. Their perspectives may be different from ours. They may have different needs, responsibilities, and dreams. And they may have different ideas about how to move forward, or even what "forward" means.

Reducing complexity to binary, either-or choices disregards the fact that there is much more to what is happening than we want to acknowledge. The survivor part of us is subconsciously aware that once we know something or have experienced or felt something, we can never again *not* know or *not* have felt or experienced it. It knows that once we allow ourselves a powerful experience or feeling, our ethical or moral self may feel compelled to step into the fray and do something about it. Because of that subconscious awareness, the survivor self doesn't want to go there. Taking action is way too threatening. The survivor self desperately wants to be in control of what is happening to us. Yet it's impossible to be in control when everything is moving and shifting. The metaphor of "herding cats" comes to mind! So the survival self prefers to foster the illusion of an over-simplified, either-or world.

However, the more attached we become to an over-simplified, either-or perception of reality, whether as individuals or societies, the greater the danger that our situation will devolve into chaos. When we don't acknowledge what is boiling under the surface, the situation becomes a pressure cooker. If there is no release for the built-up steam, the cooker will explode.

This is exactly what is happening now. In the Great Breaking Open, the pressure in the cooker is the human spirit's demand to be seen, heard, honored, respected, and connected to a greater whole. The pressure inside the cooker is cracking open the pot. The human spirit is breaking through, and right now, it's messy.

As we talked about at the end of Chapter 2, the Great Breaking Open is calling us to stretch the very fiber of our being to discover the bigger dream that is waiting for us. We have come to a critical choice point: Will we continue to take hard stances against one another? Will we keep holding on tightly to "us"—how we think, what we want, and the lives we have carefully crafted and protected—and vilifying "them"? Or will we pause, acknowledge the deep complexity of our situations and circumstances, take time to be curious and explore, and ask, "What wants to happen?"

In the simplest terms: Will we start working *with* what is breaking open, or will we continue to push *against* it and make futile attempts at "fixing" it?

We can no longer afford to pretend that the Great Breaking Open isn't happening. There is no "going back to how it was." As the saying goes, the cat is out of the bag. Denying the complexity of our circumstances by taking artificially simple, either-or, us-versus-them approaches will lead us further into chaos—a complete lack of order, structure, direction, and meaning. And the deeper we go into chaos in any system, whether that system is a family, a community, a company, a country, or the whole world, the harder it becomes to create stability. Without a minimum level of stability and safety and a sense of direction, fear reigns, and we become increasingly isolated from one another. No one can survive in isolation; much less, thrive.

So how do we move forward? An important next step, both as individuals and as a society, is to stop dumbing down what is happening in an attempt to make it more palatable or to fit the narrative of our own agenda. It's time to openly acknowledge that we are living in an unpredictable, volatile, complex system. Furthermore, it's time to acknowledge that what makes the system unpredictable and volatile is not just the many events or circumstances that we are experiencing; it's the myriad of swirling and conflicting human feelings, emotions, opinions, beliefs, desires, and dreams that are both cause and effect of what is happening.

Secondly, we can practice being fully present as we look at *and* feel into the many layers of complexity within our situations and circumstances. We can practice restraint from rushing in to solve or fix anything. We can step beyond "what I want" into "what wants to happen" for the greater good of all. We can practice sensing and intuiting the bigger picture and tap into a bigger dream for our world—a dream that is waiting just beyond the boundaries of our current imagination—and remain focused on the dream long enough for it to start showing us the way forward.

We can also practice new ways of listening and observing. Unfortunately, we have fallen into the trap of listening and observing to find out whether the other person or group is one of "us" or one of "them." Instead, we can listen and observe to learn, without judgment of right or wrong, good or bad. We can listen with the intention to learn and discover, and to deepen our understanding, instead of listening to affirm our own points of view.

Listening to learn takes much more focus and discipline than listening just to find out whether or not the other person agrees with us. It takes commitment and practice to open our hearts and minds to someone else's reality, especially when their perception of what is happening is different from our own. It takes both attention and clear *in*tention to tap into what wants to happen in the circumstances and situations of our lives, both individually and collectively.

Something new is desperately trying to happen in our world. The way forward is a step-by-step process of discovery. A new world is calling out to us. It's up to us to stretch the limits of our imagination so that we can dream it into being. No one person, philosophy, belief, or organization has the whole picture of that dream. It will take all of us dreaming together to sense it, feel it, and bring it into form.

As the dream begins to reveal itself, *it will show us* how to move forward. However, it may not show us a full-blown plan or blueprint. More often, it will only show us a next step. When we have taken that step, it will show us the next one. This is quickly becoming the new normal. In this complex world, we will only see one or two steps ahead on our path at any particular time.

Finding our way forward is also a co-creative process. As we take steps forward in response to the dream, the dream will also keep evolving in response to our commitment and action. Let's do another little mini-coaching session to help you stretch your imagination. You will find a video version of this mini-session at TransformationalPresenceBook.com.

Consider a polarizing situation or issue that has been getting your attention lately. It might be a personal or professional issue, or it might be on the political or global level. Pause for a moment to choose what you will explore in this mini-coaching session.

When you have your topic, imagine that the two sides or choices are floating out in front of you, one to the left and one to the right. Then imagine a line between them. Feel the tension and pressure in that line between the two sides. You don't have to do anything about that tension or pressure. Just be aware of it. Take your time before continuing on.

Now imagine that out beyond that line, there is another possibility that you and the people involved haven't yet considered. There is something new that wants to emerge from this situation. The greater the tension between the opposite sides, the more powerful the new vision is likely to be. Trust that, and let the potential that lies beyond the conflict reveal itself.

It might show itself to you as an image, or you might hear it as a sound or a word. Or you might sense it as energy. There is no right or wrong way. Again, take your time.

As you start to perceive it, literally stand up and walk forward through the line between the opposing sides and into that new possibility. Stand in it. Feel it, sense it, and listen to it. Resist the temptation to judge it or talk to it and instead learn from it. Be receptive. Breathe into it and let it show you your next step. And then take that next step today.

∽

Learning to live, lead, and serve within complexity is essential if we are going to create a world that works. In the *Frameworks* book, we work extensively with Dave Snowden's Cynefin Framework as well as many other tools to expand your skills and capacities for navigating, leading, and serving in today's rapidly changing world. You will also find many supportive resources at TransformationalPresenceBook.com.

In the next two chapters, we explore an emerging paradigm of leadership that embodies all that we have talked about in this book thus far, and put it into practice.

CHAPTER 9

TransformAction:
A New Kind of Leadership

He who cannot be a good follower cannot be a good leader.

—Aristotle

EARLY IN MY PROFESSIONAL LIFE, I was taught that there were three stages to becoming a leader. The first stage was to follow a leader, the second was to become a leader of your own life, and the third was to lead others. This simple outline made complete sense to me at the time. You follow others and learn. In time, you start to make choices and decisions for yourself. And then you begin to lead or influence others. I also soon realized that we cycle through these stages many times throughout our lives.

However, my work with Transformational Presence has given me a deeper understanding of these stages of leadership development. Furthermore, I sense that a fourth stage is now emerging on the periphery of conscious leadership awareness. It's this deeper understanding of leadership development and the emerging fourth stage that has inspired this book.

Let's go back and walk through each stage from the perspective of Transformational Presence.

The first stage, following a leader, might appear at first glance to be only about following. Yet from a Transformational Presence perspective, choosing whom you will follow or to what philosophies you will subscribe is also an act of leadership.

The first Principle of Transformational Presence that we explored in Chapter 4 tells us that everything is energy in motion. If everything is energy, then so are our thoughts and intentions. Therefore, when you choose to follow a particular person or philosophy, you are, in effect, *endorsing* that person or philosophy. You are sending a message that there is something about this person or philosophy that you believe in—that this is a philosophy that others may want to consider. So, from this perspective, choosing which leaders and which philosophies you will follow can be an act of leadership and influence.

The second stage of leadership is to become the leader of your own life. This is a natural part of a healthy growing-up process. Yet self-leadership is a life-long learning process of growing into who we really are and the gifts and talents we have to share. Throughout our lives, we continue to meet challenges and opportunities that require us to show up and step forward in new ways as the leaders of our own lives.

At some point, we may even feel called to take a completely new direction, at least as it may appear on the surface. Yet somehow inside, we recognize that what is pulling us in this new direction has always been there. As we grow and develop, so does our understanding of who we are and of our potential. Certainly in my own life, there have been several significant turning points when I realized that living into the next iteration of my evolving potential was going to require stepping up to new level of self-responsibility and leadership. For many of us, developing the confidence, courage, and strength it takes to fully live the life we feel called to live is, in fact, a life-long journey. The process of becoming the leader of your own life can bring you face-to-face with the situations or relationships in which you have given your power away—where you have allowed other people, circumstances, relationships, your bosses or companies, your religion or spiritual community, or perhaps even the societal norms in your country, to dictate how you show up to life and the choices you make. There may have been very good reasons for those choices. Yet at some point, many of us arrive at the question: Am I truly the leader of my own life, or am I primarily following someone else's lead or someone else's vision or dream?

Whatever your answer to that question may be, it is important to recognize whether or not your choices are working for you and for the people you care about. Are your choices supporting you to be who you are truly called to be and to do what you are here to do? Or are your choices keeping you from living into your greatest potential? What do you choose now? These are the big questions of this second phase.

If you have come this far in this book, there is a good chance that you have stepped on into the third stage of leadership—leading others. Some of us made a conscious choice to step into this third stage for a particular reason and with a certain intention. Others of us suddenly found ourselves thrust into leadership roles by other people or by particular circumstances—situations in our families, in our companies or organizations, or in our communities or larger societies.

This third stage of leadership development brings new levels of responsibility, as well as new expectations, both from self and from others. Each person has his or her own sense of what a leader is and does. This third stage often includes new (and sometimes steep!) learning curves about relationships, teamwork, delegating responsibility, supporting others to be the best they can be, creating visions and enrolling others in those visions, and leading people forward. The most dynamic and effective leaders never stop learning. And the more quickly leaders are able to learn and adapt in today's complex world, the more successful they will be.

Development in this third stage may be ongoing for the rest of our lives. Traditionally, the further up the leadership ladder you climb, the more intricate and complex leadership becomes. Each successive level brings new learning, new opportunities, and new growth.

However, a fourth stage of leadership development is now beginning to emerge. This fourth stage takes us full circle back to following. The difference is that this phase is not about following a person or a philosophy; it's about *following the emerging potential.* In this emerging fourth stage, the leader learns to tap into the energy of what is unfolding—to peer deep into the present situation or circumstance and sense or intuit the signals and messages that can show what wants to happen in the bigger picture, as well as where to go and what to do next. The leader learns that, if he or she will pay attention, the situation itself will reveal the shift that wants to happen, the breakthrough that is rising to the surface, or the new creation that is ready to emerge. The potential that is waiting to unfold is hidden within the present situation, and is often a seed of the future.

Related to the four stages of leadership development is our relationship to power. At the most basic level of awareness, we might think of power as having *power over* something or someone else, or someone or something else having power over us. From this perspective, it would seem that whoever has the power is in control.

As we mature in our relationship to power, we open to the possibility and potential available through *power with*. We begin to desire and create a sense of shared power with others, whether that is shared power in a personal or work relationship, or shared power between companies, organizations, or even countries. Decisions and choices are made together, actions are agreed upon before they are taken, and there is a sense of equality between those involved. This more mature perspective of power corresponds to the higher levels of awareness that evolve through more progressive and innovative styles of third-stage leadership development.

The fourth stage of leadership development invites us beyond *power with* to a still higher awareness—a realization that the greatest and most authentic power lies not with a person or organization, but within the greater potential that wants to unfold through a particular project, vision, situation, group, team, family, or even country. The potential is a wave of energy. Fourth-stage leaders not only follow the *energy* of the potential; they also recognize and acknowledge that *the wave of the potential—what wants to happen—is where the real power is.*

As an example, since 2015 at the Center for Transformational Presence, we have sensed that our work was taking on a life of its own. Each successive year, we have received more invitations for programs, workshops, and speaking engagements from new countries and companies. We are very conscious of *following* the energy and potential—listening, sensing, and intuiting what it is asking us for—rather than trying to lead the potential and possibilities. While we are constantly creating new programs and expanding our virtual learning opportunities, what we create is in response to what we sense that the leading edge of consciousness is asking us for next.

We think of our approach not so much as being proactive, but rather as being fully engaged with the emerging potential and following its lead. And we keep learning and making adjustments to our strategies and process as we go. We are aware that there is a wave of energy carrying us. Our job is to keep paying attention and letting it show us the way forward. We make missteps at times, yet when we do, we can usually see what it was that we weren't paying close enough attention to. We are learning as we go.

Fourth-stage leaders trust that the wave of power created by the potential will carry and support them and the project or initiative. Their job is to ride that wave and trust that if they listen, sense, and intuit what wants to happen, and then say "Yes" to what the potential is asking of them, the wave of energy that can carry the project forward will also carry them.

Transformational Presence is the full embodiment of this emerging fourth stage of leadership. This is the leadership that is necessary for navigating complexity and the unknown territories we increasingly find ourselves in. At the root of your own Transformational Presence is who you are at your core—your fundamental worldview or how you look at things, your authenticity and honesty in your dealings with others, and your deep respect and appreciation for life.

Yet Transformational Presence is about much more than just being authentic and honest. As we've said, it's a skill set. It's about your capacities for Whole-Mind Thinking and Whole-Being Awareness. It's about your capacities for sensing and intuiting the big-picture view of what is happening, recognizing emerging patterns, tapping into the hidden potential, and *letting it show you* the next step to keep moving forward.

This fourth stage invites us into a new kind of leadership for our time. We need to be not just transactional or transformational leaders; we need to be *TransformActional.* We need to be leaders who embody Transformational Presence *and* move into action. We need to *be* transformation in action.

Early on in our work at the Center for Transformational Presence, we recognized a distinction between **transactional** and **transformational** approaches to leadership and coaching. In a **transactional** approach, the intention is simple: get a result or accomplish a goal. The focus tends to be on short-term problem solving and solutions. There are certainly times when we just need to get the job done. A transactional approach works best when applied to complicated situations and circumstances.

However, as complexity has increasingly become the norm, a **transformational** approach is usually more effective and productive. While we do ultimately need to take an action and move the situation forward, a **transformational** approach begins with paying attention to all of the signals and messages to discover what wants to happen in the big picture. A **transformational** approach takes a Longpath view, seeing and sensing what is happening within a larger context. As we sense what wants to happen, we explore the shifts in perception and understanding that are needed to allow us to create effective changes and results that will lift the situation up and carry us forward. And then we take action that is aligned with our discoveries and perceptions. A **transformational** approach can include getting **transactions** accomplished. However, a **transactional** approach will rarely also include broader scale **transformation**.

Several years ago, I began sensing that there was a third approach that now wanted to come to life—something beyond the duality of **transactional** and **transformational**. One summer morning while meditating beside Chautauqua Lake in western New York, I intuitively heard the word *TransformAction*. At first I laughed at this new made-up word, yet almost immediately, I sensed there was something to it.

As I kept listening and sensing into this new concept of *TransformAction*, I began to understand it as the ability to learn a new skill, gain a new insight, or transform understanding, and immediately sense a new path or direction or a next step and move into action. *TransformAction* is transformation in action. There is no gap between learning and application. Insight and action become one gesture.

Entrepreneurs, and social entrepreneurs in particular, are perhaps our best models for this already. They sense a need in the society or marketplace and respond quickly to fill that need. They are not afraid to take risks or make mistakes. They often have no idea how to do much of what they do before they do it. They just start and find their way as they go. They transform their own belief systems and practices, and they often contribute to the transformation of a certain segment of society or of the marketplace.

As I have embodied *TransformAction* in my own life and work, I've discovered five core capacities needed for *TransformActional Leadership:*

1) **Engaging multiple levels of awareness.** *TransformAction* requires expansive awareness of what is obvious as well as what is hidden, awareness of what is happening around us as well as within us, and awareness of the personal presence we are bringing to the moment.

2) **Understanding how life works as energy in motion.** We began this discussion in Chapter 4.

3) **Practicing discovery, creativity, and innovation.** *TransformAction* is a process of "dancing in the moment," as they might say in the coaching world, or "thinking on your feet," as it might be called in the business world, and immediately responding in ways that build forward momentum.

4) **Supporting others without entanglement.** Working in complexity and the uncertainty and volatility that can come with it can be frustrating and challenging, both for us and for the people that we lead and serve. *TransformAction* requires a great capacity for being fully present and engaged with whatever is going on without getting emotionally caught up in feelings and frustrations. One of the hallmarks of the Transformational Presence approach is being able to hold situations lightly, even when facing great difficulty.

5) **Meeting whatever comes from a place of clarity, trust, and confidence.** This does not necessarily mean that you know what to do! It means that you have grown confident that if you pay attention, listen, observe, and sense with your intuitive thinking skills, you will find your next steps.

The exercises and tools in the companion *Frameworks* book and the resources you will find at Transformational-PresenceBook.com are designed to help you develop and expand these five capacities within yourself and the people you serve.

These core capacities equip us to live, lead, coach, and serve through the simple yet powerful Transformational Presence model that we first introduced in Chapter 3:

Opportunity → Presence → Action

This model carries over as the essence of *TransformAction* as well. However, *TransformAction* takes it to a new level. The three steps now happen almost simultaneously. We sense the opportunity, allow the opportunity to show us how we can best show up for greatest impact, and step into the action that we sense the opportunity is asking for, all at the same time. There is no gap between awareness and action.

The big question: How do we do that? In the next chapter we will explore four modern-day archetypes that can help us put that model into everyday practice and bring *TransformActional Leadership* to life.

CHAPTER 10

Becoming *TransformActional* Leaders: Four Modern-Day Archetypes Show Us the Way

To innovate you need more than rote knowledge.
You need a trained imagination.

—Martha Nussbaum, American philosopher
Professor of Law and Ethics at the University of Chicago

IN THE FIRST CHAPTER, WE introduced the Japanese concept of *kokoro*, referring to the alignment needed within ourselves in order to accomplish a goal or bring a vision to life. We asked two important questions for our time:

1. Who do we need to be in order to make the difference we are here to make?

2. What skills, tools, approaches, awareness, and capacities do we need within us as the people who will facilitate transformation going forward?

As I sat with these questions within the context of *TransformAction*, I began seeking a clear and simple way to embody this approach. Intuitively, I heard four words: **Seer, Explorer, Co-Creator,** and **Ambassador.**

Pondering those four words and what they represented, I began to recognize each one as a modern-day archetype symbolizing a particular set of qualities and skills. Although I hadn't recognized them before, I realized that these four archetypes had always been the foundation of Transformational Presence. Furthermore, I recognized that as we embody these archetypes as leaders, coaches, and people committed to making a difference, *TransformAction* can be a prototype for this emerging fourth stage of leadership—a leadership that truly can support us in creating a world that works.

In that spirit, I began inviting these four archetypes— the **Seer,** the **Explorer,** the **Co-Creator,** and the **Ambassador**—to talk to me. I asked them to show themselves to me as if I were meeting them for the very first time. I invited them to become my teachers and show me tools and frameworks that could help us embody the qualities that these archetypes represented. Within just a few hours, the archetypes transformed my understanding of who we need to be as leaders in a world that works for all. To my great delight, fourth-stage or *TransformActional* Leadership was already being prototyped in my awareness through this exploration.

In this chapter, I will briefly introduce each archetype, and then go into a more in-depth discussion of each one. The practical and immediately applicable tools, models, and frameworks in the *Tools, Skills, and Frameworks* book and on TransformationalPresenceBook.com will help you develop the skills and capacities of each of the archetypes.

The **Seer** sees beneath the surface and senses beyond the

obvious to perceive and understand what others do not. The Seer also understands how life works as energy in motion and looks beyond the "form" of what is happening to the energy that has created that form. The skills associated with the Seer are necessary for the full development of the other three archetypes within us.

The **Explorer** is willing to go places he or she has never been before. The Explorer is a master at navigating unknown territory, not because he or she knows all the answers or "how to get there," but rather because he or she has lots of tools and skills to find the path and move forward. The Explorer understands that trailblazing can be risky business, yet is necessary in order to clear a path for others and for what is waiting to emerge. The Explorer might be just as frightened by the unknown as others, yet at the same time, the call from the wilderness is too strong to resist. The Explorer also understands that the unknown not only includes places, circumstances, or situations; it also includes our inner landscape of thoughts, ideas, beliefs, emotions, and feelings.

The **Co-Creator** recognizes and acknowledges that life is a co-creative process. The Co-Creator accepts that whatever is in front of her or him—whether that is a person, a situation, or an idea—can be the next co-creative or collaborative partner. We are constantly co-creating with everything around us. The more intentional we are about that co-creation, the more we can move forward in alignment with "what wants to happen."

The **Ambassador** builds bridges of understanding and awareness. Always sensing the big-picture view, the Ambassador invites others to new ways of being and doing—new methods, new approaches, and new perspectives.

As we develop the skills and capacities of these archetypes within ourselves, and then help the people in our teams, organizations, families, or communities develop these same skills and capacities, we start to build a dynamic and positive culture. This culture is based not just on mutual respect and honest relationships, but also on intuitive thinking, creative and innovative approaches, and sustainable action. This is the beginning of prototyping *TransformActional* Leadership in our organizations and in all sectors of society.

The Seer

The real voyage of discovery consists not in seeking new landscapes, but in having new eyes.

—Marcel Proust, French writer and philosopher

Conventional wisdom tells us that in order to solve a problem, we need to figure out what isn't working and why, and then fix it. And if we don't know how, we find the expert who does. That approach often works well in complicated situations. However, as we talked about in Chapters 8 and 9, many of the challenges we face today are complex. And when working in complexity, we come back to the Transformational Presence tenet: A problem is not something to be solved; it is a message to be listened to. We have said that complex issues require a shift in *how we think* and in *how we perceive.* The first step in that shift is to learn to see and perceive in a new way.

It's been said that you can't really see something until you can forget its name. In other words, we tend to see what we expect to see. Once we have given something a name, it's hard for us to see it as anything else. When we look at a chair, we can only see a chair. However, if we stretch our imagination just a bit, the chair might also become a stepping stool. We can stand on it to get to something that before was too high for us to reach. If we look at a table, we only see a table. Yet in a child's imagination, the table might become a stage upon which to perform. Or it might become a mountain cliff off of which she could jump. Or he might drape a cloth or blanket over the table and the space underneath becomes a cave.

Chances are, at some point in your playful life, a table has become a stage or a cave, or you have stood on a chair. Or perhaps in your childhood, a sofa became a dragon, or a swiveling chair became a merry-go-round. In those moments, there were no limits or boundaries in your imagination or thinking. When we let go of what we "know" things to be, they can become something else. New possibilities can then arise.

Unfortunately, most of us tend to "look" but not "see." We tend to see what we are thinking already. We see what we have context or understanding for. We see what we look for. We see concepts, but not details, patterns, or energy. We see a tree, yet we don't notice that it is an *oak* tree with particular patterns in the leaves and the bark. We see several chairs in a room, yet we don't notice that one has blue tapestry upholstery and wooden arms while another is green with yellow trim, and yet another has a carved pattern in the wooden back. Or we see a room, yet we don't notice that one of the walls is a slightly different color than the others. We may not notice that the energy in one room of a house or office feels open and welcoming while another room feels sterile and cold.

The first of the four archetypes that can help us prototype *TransformActional* Leadership is the **Seer.** A Seer is one who uses "inner sight" or "intuitive sight" to see beyond the limits of conditioned thought patterns. The Seer perceives what others do not, seeing and sensing patterns, perceiving energy in relationships, and intuiting how one thing fits together with another. A Seer looks beyond the obvious, reads energy, and recognizes trends and probabilities. While some might think of a Seer as one who can foretell the future, a Seer is actually one who is able to peer deep into the present moment to find the essence of what is happening or the greatest potential that is waiting to unfold.

The **Seer** understands that first fundamental principle of how the world works: Everything is energy in motion, part of a larger process unfolding. Therefore, the Seer looks beneath the surface of circumstances or situations to sense where energy is moving and where it is stuck. The Seer is looking for the bigger picture, recognizing that whatever is happening is actually a part of a larger unfolding process. The Seer also understands that nothing happens on its own without relationship to something else. Nothing exists in isolation. Everything exists as a part of a larger flow.

The **Seer** understands that because everything is fundamentally energy in motion, everything is constantly changing. Nothing is fixed or permanent. Change, transformation, and evolution are a part of the natural flow of life. Therefore, the Seer looks at circumstances and situations as existing within a changing and evolutionary process and gathers insight from what he or she observes.

The **Seer** understands that form follows energy—that circumstances and situations are manifestations of energy patterns. Therefore, the Seer knows that the most efficient, effective, and sustainable way to create lasting change is to work first at the energy level—to sense what wants to happen at the energy level and then help facilitate those shifts. The circumstance or situation can then change in its own organic and natural way. Again, form follows energy.

In summary, a **Seer**:

- Perceives beyond the obvious to discover or recognize things that others do not

- Engages both the inner and outer senses

- Looks for patterns and energy textures within situations and circumstances

- Intuits how one thing fits together with another

- Peers deep into the present moment to discover the future that is waiting to unfold

Developing your **Seer** skills starts with being open and curious. Here are a few guidelines that can help you start developing these skills right away:

- Step beyond your own context. Let things show themselves to you on their own terms. Set aside your own interpretations of what is happening and of what people say and do and see what else there might be to discover.

- Allow what you are looking at or experiencing to surprise you—to be different from what you might have expected.

- Practice Whole-Mind Thinking and Whole-Being Awareness (Chapter 6) to sense beyond the limits of your habitual thinking, your present knowledge, and your accepted beliefs.

If you wish to further develop and refine your **Seer** skills, you will find many practical exercises and tools in the *Frameworks* book that you can start using immediately in your life and work.

The Explorer

In times of change, learners inherit the earth,
while the learned find themselves beautifully equipped
to deal with a world that no longer exists.

—Eric Hoffer, American moral and social philosopher

In our VUCA world, we're facing both challenges and opportunities that we've never met before. Effective leadership for today and tomorrow often means walking into the unknown and trusting that, even though we don't know what we are doing or where we are going, somehow we will find each next step at the right time. This is the realm of the **Explorer**.

Explorers accept not having answers and not knowing "how" before they move forward. When doing something for the first time or creating something new, they have no expectation of knowing how to do it ahead of time. They use their **Seer** skills to *discover* each new step as it comes. They trust that a plan will reveal itself as they move forward. Only after they have accomplished their goal or vision are they able to look back and recognize how they did it.

TransformActional Leadership is an ongoing process of discovery, learning and creating as we go. With today's complex challenges, there are rarely blueprints or master plans to follow. Our job is to look deep into the circumstance or situation **(Seer)** to recognize the potential waiting to unfold, explore the terrain, sense each next step as it comes, and follow through with appropriate action or response.

In our mainstream culture, we have been conditioned to view "not knowing" as a sign of incompetence in leadership. We've created an expectation that the leader needs to have the answers. Many of us were taught that we should "know how to do it" or know every detail of where we are going before we take the first step. The intellect is eager to reinforce this conditioning because when we know from the beginning how to accomplish the task at hand, the intellect feels more secure and less vulnerable.

Explorers approach life with an attitude of curiosity and a willingness to proceed even when they don't know how. When we only do things that we know how to do and are not willing to move forward until we've answered every question, we will, in the end, stay where we are. In other words, we will stay in our comfort zone—in known territory. Staying in known territory leads to re-creating some version of the past over and over again. Meanwhile, the world is moving on. As Eric Hoffer said in the quote at the beginning of this section, we get better and better at living in a world that no longer exists.

A big part of our job as **Explorers** is to encourage and support a culture of discovery, creativity, and innovation among the people we serve—a culture that is inspired and informed by what we see and by what we discover together as we go. The best possible future will show itself to us if we are willing to explore with an open mind and heart.

Seasoned **Explorers** trust that as they explore unknown territory, signs will appear to show them where to go next. They recognize the importance of paying attention on many levels of awareness—of using all of their intuitive senses. They hone their Whole-Mind Thinking and Whole-Being Awareness skills. They understand that the seeds of the future are planted in the present, and that, if they will pay attention, the future will show them the way forward.

In alignment with Eric Hoffer's words, business innovator Nilofer Merchant said:

> *When a society accepts the practices, methods, and measures*
> *of the 20th century to conceive the 21st century, failure is inevitable.*
> *In order to consider new ideas you have to be willing to let go*
> *of ones that no longer serve you.*

This brings us to the first skill of the **Explorer**—learning forward. Most of us have been conditioned to "learn backwards." In other words, when we learn something new, whether consciously or unconsciously, we interpret and assimilate that new information within the context of our previous knowledge and experience. The meaning we give to our new experiences is based on our past. If the new learning affirms or is congruent with what we already know, we are likely to accept it and work with it.

However, if it contradicts our past experience or understanding, or if we don't already have a context in which to put the new information, we may reject it. Our openness to learn something completely new or to perceive something in a radically different way is often limited by what we already know or have experienced. When we "learn backwards," our discovery and interpretation of the moment is limited by the structures and contexts of our current knowledge.

"Learning forward" means that we meet circumstances and situations on their own terms. Understanding that the world is evolving rapidly, we recognize that the present and future may be operating from a different set of rules and conditions than what we have known in the past. Therefore, *we let life show itself to us* rather than assuming that we know what something is or what the outcome of a situation will be before we've actually experienced it. We allow ourselves to experience something fully before we give it meaning or interpretation. We meet new situations and circumstances with an open mind and heart—with curiosity. We live in an attitude of discovery, treating each experience and situation as something new with its own set of messages and opportunities.

Learning forward means accepting what we are learning as a new context or base. Some of our past knowledge, experience, beliefs, and practices will continue to serve us in this new context, and some may no longer be relevant. We let go of what is no longer relevant and continue exploring forward, learning the new rules as we go.

Learning forward is as important for organizations as it is for individuals. A global services company invited me to help them explore a new product idea. They envisioned an innovative service that would inspire and support transformational leadership in business in new ways. They were incredibly excited about the new possibilities for their customers as well as for themselves as a company. They asked me to join their leadership team on an exploration and strategy retreat to find their next steps.

At one point mid-way through our process, I realized that they were trying to fit their innovative new idea into an old service model. They were, in effect, learning backwards. Their old model was closely tied to their core identity as a company and the unique ways in which they offered their services. However, that old model, and maybe even how they saw themselves as a company, was too confining for the new idea.

At the same time, I knew it would be much more powerful for them if they discovered the deeper layers of what was happening themselves instead of me simply sharing my observation. Then it would belong to them. Learning by discovery is much more effective and impactful than simply being told by someone else.

I invited the team into an exercise to explore where they were in that moment, both in terms of what they had accomplished thus far, as well as the next steps they were trying to take. I invited them to acknowledge both their excitement and their frustration—what was working well as well as ways in which they felt stuck.

From there, we stepped onto a timeline. We stepped back in time to visit a situation in their past that felt relevant to their current circumstance. We explored what was important about that past time and experience and what they remembered learning in that moment. We acknowledged that some of that learning might support them in their present circumstance, while at the same time, some of what they learned then was perhaps no longer relevant to their new concept. From the past, we brought forward to the present the learning that could actually serve them today, and left the rest behind.

Already, there was an excitement in the group as they began to sense new pathways in front of them. However, there was still another step to go. We looked out into the future to sense what was calling them forward. While each person sensed something a little different, they discovered as a group that there were a couple of common themes. As we listened together to those common themes, the team began to discover the ways in which their old structure was holding them back. Within an hour, they had released this new project from the confines of their old model, setting themselves and the project free to take on a new life. It was an extraordinary turning point in the project development.

Learning backward is static. It puts learning and experiences into boxes and categories, immediately labeling or interpreting them to fit into pre-existing models and structures. In contrast, learning forward is dynamic, generative, and ever-evolving. There is a constant sense of movement and flow, sometimes gentle and easy, while at other times, fast and furious.

Learning forward generates momentum, each discovery leading to another. It opens up a bigger-picture view, and often inspires outcomes even greater than your initial vision or project. It can offer a broader perspective on your project and how it fits into a larger evolutionary flow within your organization and/or the people involved. As you learn forward, you help propel the mass consciousness forward. Learning forward is a critical **Explorer** skill in *Transform-Actional* leadership.

You will find a full step-by-step script for the "Learning Forward" exercise in the *Frameworks* book, as well as many other **Explorer** tools and skills to support you and the people and organizations you serve.

The **Seer** and **Explorer** qualities and skills are the life-blood of leading within complexity and navigating the unknown and unexpected. Embodying these archetypes, you get better and better at noticing the signals, sensing the messages, and following each next step. Through approaching both your challenges and opportunities with the attitudes, skills, awareness, and tools of these two archetypes, and by supporting the people you serve to do the same, you lay a foundation for a *TransformActional* culture.

As we refine our skills as **Seers** and **Explorers**, we naturally start to become **Co-Creators**. We begin engaging with everything and everyone around us in new ways, and new doors continue to open.

The Co-Creator

I begin with an idea, and then it becomes something else.

—Pablo Picasso

Whether or not we acknowledge it, life is an ongoing co-creative process with the people, ideas, beliefs, and circumstances around us. For many people, this is an unconscious process. They simply allow life's circumstances and situations to create their present and future. The problem with this approach is that they also sometimes feel powerless to create something different than what is happening.

However, there is another way. We can make a conscious choice to be engaged and intentional in the co-creation process. In the context of *TransformAction*, this means sensing the potential waiting to unfold within a circumstance, situation, or project, and responding immediately in the most appropriate ways to who it is asking us to be and what it is asking us to do.

We have spoken about this already in Chapter 4 when we talked about the second fundamental principle of Transformational Presence: Energy cannot be created or destroyed; it can only be transformed. We also introduced the concept of "Push Against – Flow With" in that chapter. As a review, this concept reminds us that when we accept our circumstance and work with it instead of push against it, things are a lot easier. We may not like what is happening. Yet if we will step beyond our judgments and opinions, and accept that, at least for the moment, this is our circumstance, we can move forward. When we are willing to *work with it*, there is usually a much better chance that we can co-create something new.

You will also remember the distinction between "flow with" and "go with the flow." Intuiting the hidden message and potential is what makes "flow with" different from just giving up or giving in to whatever is happening. "Flow with," in this context, means to sense the greatest potential waiting to unfold in service of all involved, and then to do your part to steward that potential into reality. "What *is* happening" may not be leading you in a direction that serves the greatest possible outcome. Yet as a **Seer**, you recognize that this is not truly what *wants* to happen for a greater good. Using your **Seer** and **Explorer** skills, you can sense the emerging potential and become a steward for it, helping it unfold from potential into tangible reality.

Co-creation is a "flow with" process. Awareness of how we are approaching our situations is an important first step.

Are we "pushing against" what we don't want or what is not working, or are we "flowing with" what wants to happen?

The basic questions we ask in response to what is happening are already steering us towards one approach or the other. When our first questions are, "How do we fix this?" or "What's our plan?"—questions that take us right away to working with the form instead of the energy—we are heading down a "push against" path. However, when our first questions are, "What wants to happen?" or "Where is the energy moving, and where is it stuck?" or "What is this situation trying to show us?"—questions that go straight to the energy—we are heading down a "flow with" path.

"Flow with" can happen when we stay in discovery, engaging all of our inner and outer senses and all of our channels of awareness. Co-creation begins by "tuning in" to our co-creative partners, including the hidden messages within circumstances and situations. It requires discipline, focus, and commitment to finding the path that will create the best outcome for all.

As with the **Seer** and **Explorer**, you will find many tools and exercises to help facilitate discovery of "what wants to happen" as well as tools for expanding your capacities for co-creation, co-innovation, and collaboration in the companion *Frameworks* book.

The Ambassador

We do not think ourselves into a new way of living;
but we live ourselves into a new way of thinking.

—Father Richard Rohr, Franciscan Priest
Core Principle #8 of the Center for Action and Contemplation

TransformAction needs the full awareness of the **Seer,** the **Explorer,** and the **Co-creator.** The **Seer** perceives what is happening at the essence level and the potential that is waiting to unfold. The **Explorer** pushes the limits to find what else is there that hasn't yet been discovered. The **Co-Creator** partners with the potential and other players where appropriate to create something new.

As we refine our skills and capacities with those first three archetypes, the **Ambassador** is the natural next step. The Ambassador senses the big picture and invites others to new ways of thinking and perceiving, and to new approaches.

As **Seers, Explorers,** and **Co-Creators,** tapping into higher awareness has become a way of life for us. Thinking intuitively has become our habit. As we become **Ambassadors** of *TransformAction,* we help those we serve cross over into greatly expanded ways of living and working. We build bridges to higher levels of consciousness, whether in societies, organizations, companies, educational or healthcare systems, or governments.

Ambassadors are hosts, inviting others to discover and experience a new culture, a new way of doing something, a new way of being. Ambassadors build bridges of understanding and awareness. Often in a foreign land, they invite the people there to taste the culture and awareness of the land from which they come. The Ambassador must speak the foreign language well enough so that they can create a bridge of understanding to another place. The Ambassador puts one foot in each world and becomes the bridge to a new experience and understanding.

As **Ambassadors,** our powerful questions become invitations into new perspectives and approaches. We've said before that we don't tell those we serve *what* to think; we invite them into *new ways* of thinking. We offer them tools and skills that become bridges to new ways of perceiving and engaging both their inner and outer worlds. We invite them to *work with* whatever is in front of them rather than fight against it. We invite them to become **Seers, Explorers,** and **Co-Creators.** We invite them into their own Transformational Presence, and ultimately into *TransformAction.*

As those we serve learn to think and experience in more expanded ways, they discover what wants to happen in their circumstances and situations, as well as their next steps. In turn, they also become **Seers, Explorers,** and **Co-Creators.** And in time, they will then become **Ambassadors** for those that they serve. In this way, the mass consciousness evolves. We get to be a part of and serve that evolution.

Ambassadors can be bridges to the new language and culture of complexity. For most people, complexity is like a foreign and unknown country. Navigating the land of complexity requires a new set of skills and capacities. Ambassadors open doors of understanding and awareness.

Doing transformational work and turning that transformation into action often involves crossing over "edges." By "edge," I mean the meeting point or boundary between our comfort zone and a way of being, a place, or an action that makes us uncomfortable. Anyone who is committed to personal and professional evolution has probably crossed over edges to get to where they are now. Crossing edges is how we learn, stretch, and grow.

Ambassadors of a higher consciousness and awareness help people cross those edges. They open doors, extend invitations to new levels of presence and action, and offer an arm of support where needed. In the end, we all have to step across our edges on our own. Yet it is certainly a gift to have someone provide a steadying presence, moral support, reassurance, and encouragement.

Ambassadors also understand that we become what we create. Our creations make us who we are. Therefore, Ambassadors understand the importance of having clear intentions. Our intentions shape both our presence and our actions. Our presence and actions combine to create forms, policies, structures, and systems. In turn, we begin to shape our lives and societies around or against those forms, policies, structures, and systems. In that way, what we create turns around and creates us.

We're creating all the time. We create projects; we build businesses; we develop relationships. We tell stories, both to ourselves and to others, about who we are, about what we can and cannot do, about how life is treating us, about what happened to us in the past, and about what we see or hope for in our future. The more we tell those stories and the more energy and commitment we give to those creations, the more they, in turn, create us. From the beginning of the creative process, the process itself starts shaping our choices and decisions and the ways we engage with life, work, and relationships.

At least once in your life, you have probably experienced making a decision or taking a first step towards something new and recognized a shift within yourself as a result. Something felt different. You started showing up differently, thinking differently, and perhaps even talking about your project or idea differently.

When what we create—a project, a business, a decision, a relationship, or a story—is in alignment with our deepest values and our soul mission or life purpose, it becomes a vehicle for our own growth and development. It becomes a structure through which we can learn, evolve, and grow into our greatest potential. And it will, in some way, also serve or support those around us.

Patricia's soul mission is "I connect." Through her work, she connects people who have common interests and visions. She also connects people with charities and causes that are aligned with their missions and values. And she connects companies that have a strong social mission to a global food program. Through what she has created by living her soul mission, Patricia has grown tremendously as a high-level executive, as an entrepreneur, as a not-for-profit board member, and as a person. She has built a network of connections, and that network continues to shape who she is and what she does.

However, when what we create is *not* in alignment with our soul mission and values, a split starts to occur deep within the heart of our being. The more energy and commitment we give to that creation, similar to the gap between heart and head we talked about in Chapter 2, the gap between who we are and what we are living gets deeper and wider. Over time, we create emotional and physical constructs to protect us from the pain and dysfunction that comes from that gap. As we continue to follow the paths of our creations instead of the paths of our souls, and as those creations increasingly take over our lives, we lose our connection with our true selves.

Strongly influenced by his father, Edward dreamed of running a global company from a young age. His father taught him that you set goals in order to make money and be successful. Yet Edward had a secret passion for painting and sculpture. The more successful he became in international real estate, the less time or energy he had for his creative side. He worked hard and earned a very high salary, yet he was miserable. He didn't want to buy and sell buildings; he wanted to create artworks that would bring those spaces to life. In the end, both his business and his marriage failed. He had created a life that he resented, and that life, in turn, nearly destroyed him.

The same is true at the organizational and society levels. When what organizations or companies create is in alignment with something bigger than themselves—when it is in service of what wants to happen for a greater good—the organization contributes to creating a world that works. However, when what is created is in opposition to what wants to happen in service of a greater good, a split begins to form at the heart of the organization or society.

The **Ambassador** recognizes that we're at a crossroads on every level of society. Perhaps the most fundamental invitation right now is to be aware that everything that we create—whether in our families or in business, government, education, healthcare, or the arts—in turn, impacts who we are as a society and how we engage with one another. Going forward, it is critical that we bring conscious awareness and intention to every choice and decision we make, every new policy and structure we establish, and every new relationship in which we engage. What we create, what we choose, how we act, what we legislate, and the kinds of policies we put in place, will, in turn, shape who we are, both as societies and as individuals.

From this awareness, the **Ambassador** asks: Who do we want to be as a society? Or the even bigger question: Who are we as a society *called* to be? What are the longings deep within our collective heart—the longings that won't let go of us? What kinds of new policies, forms, and structures is the collective heart asking us to create that can, in turn, help us to live into our greatest collective potential?

From there, the **Ambassador** brings the question to the personal level: Within that greater societal picture, who do you, personally, feel called to be? What is the longing deep in your heart that won't let go of you? What kind of life, career, business, invention, service, or gift do you feel called to contribute to the world around you? What is *your* greatest potential, at least as you understand it now?

The **Ambassador** recognizes that the fastest way for individuals and organizations to reach their potential and share their gifts is to create projects and visions that require them to step into that potential, and then to get busy bringing those projects and visions to life. In the spirit of *kokoro*, they will become the people or organization that creates that. The project or vision itself will support them in becoming who they feel called to be.

These are conversations that are wanting to happen, not just for our personal fulfillment, but for the good of all. They are multi-faceted, long-term conversations. They want to happen around dinner tables, in houses of worship, in civic meetings, at social gatherings, in education halls, and in government chambers. They are Longpath conversations that evolve over time.

The **Ambassador** understands that if we create space for those conversations and invite a greater potential to lead the way, even the conversations themselves will expand how we see the world. They will start to have significant impact on the choices and decisions we make going forward. If we create space for these conversations, especially at the societal level, the conversations will begin to create us.

As we embody the qualities of the **Seer, Explorer, Co-Creator,** and **Ambassador**, we learn to intuit what wants to happen and move directly into action. We co-create with potential. We "flow with" instead of "push against." Rather than view circumstances as problems to be solved, we tap into the essence of what is happening, look for the greatest potential waiting to emerge, partner with that potential, and flow with it as it starts to unfold. We become *TransformActional* in our leadership, coaching, and service of a greater good, trusting that, if we pay attention, the potential will show us the way forward.

CHAPTER 11

TransformAction: The Way Forward

What we create is a reflection of who we are;
who we are is a reflection of what we create.
Therefore, create what you wish to become.
The attributes of our creations will become the attributes we live.

—Alan Seale

AS WE LOOK FORWARD AND consider our future, perhaps the most important question is not, "What will we create?" but rather, "Who do we wish to become?"

John Sawhill, past president of New York University and of The Nature Conservancy, wrote, "In the end, our society will be defined not only by what we create, but by what we refuse to destroy."

One way of interpreting the last part of Sawhill's statement is that we will protect that which we consider most important to us. We will not destroy that which we cherish deeply.

However, there can also be another meaning in his statement: Our society is defined not only by what we choose to create and what we choose to protect, but also by what structures, systems, practices, and beliefs we choose to transform or allow to die. Sometimes we make those choices consciously, and at other times, unconsciously.

John Sawhill's words feel particularly relevant to me as we navigate the Great Breaking Open and stretch the boundaries of our imaginations to discover the bigger dream that we spoke about in Chapter 2. Without question, dreaming a new and bigger dream will lead to the creation of new structures, forms, systems, and ways of engaging with one another. At the same time, the bigger dream will also ask us to let some of our societal systems, structures, traditions, beliefs, and practices die. If we refuse, we hold society back.

The idea of letting familiar structures and systems die can be a scary. Perhaps the scariest moment comes when we realize that we're going to have to let go of what we have known—of what is familiar—*before* we have something new to hold on to. In the midst of transitions, we don't know what we can depend on. We don't know what to trust. We don't know where to find solid ground. In fact, in these scary moments, all we actually have to rely on is the authentic power and strength within each of us that we find when we are willing to be fully open and fully real at the same time.

These kinds of bold steps can only happen within a society when enough individuals have found the courage and strength to let old structures die within their own lives and beliefs. As more individuals blaze the trail forward, at a certain point, critical mass is reached and society moves forward.

As society moves forward, even more individuals are able to find the courage to take these steps in their own lives.

Organizations and businesses follow, and the cycle continues. Individual choices and beliefs influence societal shifts and, in turn, societal shifts influence individual choices and beliefs. Step by step, the collective evolves.

Evolutionary shifts within a society take time. Dreaming, evolving, and shifting all unfold through process. Leading and supporting that process of societal change and transformation in an effective, impactful, and grace-filled way is an art. It's a balancing act between pushing the edges of what a society is comfortable with, yet not pushing people so far beyond what they know that fear takes over. Fear can keep us from making forward movement, and can even pull us backwards.

Transformational Presence and *TransformActional* Leadership are all about finding the perfect balance. It's an intricate dance. This approach is not about making things happen; it's about sensing the transformation that the societal system is ready for at the moment and creating the best possible environment for that transformation to unfold.

There is a saying, "Two steps forward; one step back." Each time we make a significant shift toward a world that works for all, some people will celebrate and others will be afraid. When the majority of people are celebrating, society is able to take another step forward. When a large number of people are afraid, society falls back a step. It's all a part of the dance. In the end, the full spectrum of feelings, emotions, and opinions of both the majority *and* minority must be acknowledged, respected, and responded to in some way. These are lessons that, hopefully, we are learning now through the Great Breaking Open.

Commitment to the bigger process is critical. Political leader and social activist Rev. William Barber, founder of the "Moral Mondays" civil rights protests, asks, "Are you committed to the movement or to the moment?"

Many "moments" have led up to the era of the Great Breaking Open. The breaking open that we are now experiencing is spawning a conscious leadership and service *movement*. Commitment to this movement will mean sticking with it through many "two steps forward and one step back" moments. It will take Longpath focus, diligence, persistence, determination, trust, faith, and courage to speak and act, sometimes in the face of risk and uncertainty.

The Great Breaking Open is a global event that is unfolding right in front of us and within us. It invites us to create new structures and systems, new paradigms and perspectives. It invites us to protect those parts of our heritage, traditions, and ethics that will support our ongoing evolution towards a world that works for all. And it invites us to transform or let die those systems and structures, paradigms and perspectives that hold us back or that support a world that only works for some. It invites us to dream a bigger dream—a dream that will continue evolving and asking us to stretch the boundaries of our imaginations over and over again.

This book has given you a foundation of understanding and awareness. The companion *Frameworks* book and the support website TransformationalPresenceBook.com will give you tools, skills, frameworks, and models that can support you in becoming a new kind of conscious leader—a *TransformActional* Leader—for our rapidly changing world. As we've said several times, the point of these two books is not to tell you or society what to do. It's to show you how to discover the potential waiting to unfold in every situation or circumstance, and then how to tap into that potential to show the path forward.

TransformAction can become a way of life. It can become our way of approaching everything from our most personal situations to our shared global opportunities and challenges. It can shape how we navigate our most important relationships, raise our children, work with colleagues, lead a project or organization, govern countries, and empower global initiatives.

TransformAction begins with intuiting what wants to happen—letting the potential show itself to us instead of assuming that we know what should be done. It means listening, sensing, intuiting on many levels of awareness all the time, and letting the potential lead the way. It means learning forward. The potential will show us how to move into action when the time is right and the pieces have come into place. This is co-creation in its highest form.

We will not create a world that works overnight. However, you might be surprised to find that transformation within your personal life and for the people that you serve can happen more quickly than you thought possible.

And for our world, don't worry about how long it will take or how we will bring that potential to reality. Just get started. Take a Longpath view. Engage others in this conversation. Keep paying attention to what the situation is asking for and say, "Yes." Be *TransformActional.* Step by step, month by month, year by year, things will change. You will make a difference, and as a result, you and your life will be different.

We are living in amazing, tumultuous, creative, uncertain, extraordinary times. Sense the potential. Let that potential show you what it needs and how to bring it to reality. Be the person it is asking you to be and take the action it asks you to take. It really is that simple. And it's how we can create a world that works.

Books

Berger, Jennifer Garvey, with Keith Johnston. *Simple Habits for Complex Times: Powerful Practices for Leaders.* Redwood City, CA: Stanford Business Books, 2016.

Childre, Doc, with Howard Martin and Donna Beech. *The HeartMath Solution.* New York: HarperCollins Publishers, 1999.

Korten, David C. *Change the Story, Change the Future: A Living Economy for a Living Earth.* Oakland: Berrett-Koehler Publishers, 2015.

Korten, David C. *The Great Turning: From Empire to Earth Community.* Oakland: Berrett-Koehler Publishers, 2007.

Macy, Joanna, with Chris Johnstone. *Active Hope: How to Face the Mess We're In without Going Crazy.* Novato, CA: New World Library, 2012.

Macy, Joanna, with Molly Young Brown. *Coming Back to Life: The Updated Guide to the Work that Reconnects.* Gabriola Island, BC, Canada: New Society Publishers, 2014.

McTaggart, Lynne. *The Field: The Quest for the Secret Force of the Universe.* New York: HarperCollins Publishers, 2002.

Newell, John Philip. *The Rebirthing of God: Christianity's Struggles for New Beginnings.* Nashville: SkyLight Paths, 2014.

De Mille, Agnes. *Martha: The Life and Work of Martha Graham.* New York: Random House, 1956.

Rohr, Richard. *The Eight Core Principles.* Cincinnati: Franciscan Media, 2013.

Seale, Alan. *Create A World That Works.* San Francisco: Red Wheel/Weiser, 2011.

Three Initiates. *The Kybalion: Hermetic Philosophy.* N.p.: Yogi Publication Society, 1940.

Wheatley, Margaret J. *Who Do We Choose To Be?: Facing Reality, Claiming Leadership, Restoring Sanity.* Oakland: Berrett-Koehler Publishers, 2017.

Audio

Whyte, David. *A Great Invitation: The Path of Risk and Revelation.* Langley, WA: Many Rivers Press, 2013.

Whyte, David. *Solace: The Art of Asking the Beautiful Question*. Langley, WA: Many Rivers Press, 2014.

Whyte, David. *What To Remember When Waking: The Disciplines of Everyday Life*. Louisville, CO: Sounds True, 2010.

Online Sources

Center for Transformational Presence—www.transformationalpresence.org

Center for Action and Contemplation, Richard Rohr, Founder—www.cac.org

Cognitive Edge, Dave Snowden, Founder—www.cognitive-edge.com

The Heartbeat of God—www.heartbeatjourney.org

HeartMath Institute—www.heartmath.org

Trace Hobson, strategic alliance partner for the Center for Transformational Presence—www.iconnectexpansion.com

Ari Wallach, futurist—www.longpath.org

THE CENTER FOR
—— TRANSFORMATIONAL PRESENCE ——

Founded by Alan Seale in 2010, the Center for Transformational Presence is a global discovery, learning, and transformation environment for leaders, coaches, teachers, visionaries, social entrepreneurs, managers, parents, healthcare professionals, educators, artists, politicians, public servants, and anyone who wants to make a difference in the world.

We help you and your organization create wholeness, meaning, direction, sense of purpose, and sustainable action so that you can realize your greatest potential and make the contribution to the world that you are here to make.

Why? Our mission is simple: We create a world that works.

How? Through virtual learning and coaching as well as in-person workshops and development programs, we offer a full Transformational Presence toolkit and skill set—simple and practical yet incredibly powerful tools and approaches that will build and expand your capacities for awareness, perception, understanding, compassion, and effective action.

Join us!

TransformationalPresence.org

ACKNOWLEDGMENTS

Every book that I have written has had its own unique journey and process. However, none has felt as urgent and timely as this one. The writing process has been fierce and relentless. The book grabbed hold of me and would not let go. And for that I am grateful. The work of Transformational Presence continues to be my greatest teacher. I feel blessed that this work chose me.

Thank you to the Transformational Presence community for your deep commitment to this work. I dedicate this book to you. Through your participation and engagement in the Transformational Presence Leadership and Coaching development programs as well as the "Soul Mission * Life Vision" and "Manifestation Wheel" workshops, masterclasses, personal coaching, monthly community calls, and our Transformational Presence Global Summits and Global Leadership Gatherings, you have contributed immeasurably to the evolution of this work.

Throughout the writing process, I have been grateful for the editing and content support of Cynthia Smith, Peggy MacArthur, Johnathon Pape, and Trace Hobson. Your support through various iterations of the manuscript was invaluable. Thank you.

Thank you also to readers of the manuscript, giving me feedforward and encouragement at various stages of the writing process: Kim Adams, Jonathan Anderson, Jo Boniszewski, Mark Braber, Joan Diver, Amy Herrboldt, Rebecca Johns, Gabriella van Rooij, and Judy Schnitger.

Thank you to my partner in life, Johnathon Pape, for your love, support, and encouragement for all that I am and for my walk in the world. I am incredibly blessed to share my life with you.

Finally, to all of you who read this book and embody its principles, thank you for all that you are and all that you do to make a difference and to help create a world that works.

ABOUT THE AUTHOR

Photo credit: Nic Askew

ALAN SEALE is an inspirational speaker, transformation catalyst, master teacher and mentor to leaders and coaches around the world, and the founder of the Center for Transformational Presence. Graduates from his programs come from more than 30 countries. His books have been published in six languages.

Alan has been a keynote speaker for International Coach Federation (ICF) global conferences, both in-person and via streaming video. He has also served as keynote speaker for ICF Regional Conferences in the U.K., Sweden, Romania, Spain, and Latin America, as well as for leadership and spirituality conferences in the United States and Canada. Truly a global coach, Alan currently serves clients from five continents.

Intuitive Living: A Sacred Path (winner of the Coalition of Visionary Resources Award for Best Book in Spiritualtiy in 2001)

Soul Mission, Life Vision

The Manifestation Wheel: A Practical Process for Creating Miracles

The Power of Your Presence: A Daily Workout For Your Soul

Create A World That Works: Tools for Personal and Global Transformation